# Lakes Region Culinary Institute

## Cookbook

*Recipes from the cooking school with wine pairings*

First Edition
August 2011

*for Helga*

By Ronald W. Collins
Executive Chef
Lakes region Culinary Institute
Hebron, New Hampshire

© 2011 Ronald W. Collins, all rights reserved

**Collins Publishing**

O'CULLANE (COLLINS)

ISBN-13: 978-1463744298
ISBN-10: 1463744293

# Contents

Conversions ................................................ 8
Introduction: ............................................... 9
    Preface by Ronald Collins ........................ 9
    Lakes Region Culinary Institute ................ 10
Appetizers ................................................ 11
    Roasted Peppers with Prosciutto and Fontina .... 12
    Cherry Tomatoes Stuffed with Spanish Olive Tapenade ............................................. 13
    Blue Cheese & Walnut Coated Cherry Tomatoes ........................................... 14
    Mushroom Puffs .................................. 15
    Shrimp Mozambique ............................... 16
    Blue Cheese Shortbreads with Walnuts and Chutney ............................................. 17
    Shrimp Scampi Quesadillas ....................... 19
    Rosemary and Parmesan Savories ................. 20
    Grilled Vegetable Pita Pizzas with Sun Dried Tomato Pesto ......................................... 21
        Sun Dried Tomato Pesto ...................... 22
        Note on Parmesan Cheese .................... 23
    Roast Beef & Gorgonzola Salad .................. 25
    Asian Beef Skewers .............................. 26
    Black Bean & Garlic Hummus ..................... 27
        Note on Garlic ............................. 28
        Note: Green Shoots in Garlic? .............. 29
        Note on Black Olives ....................... 29
    Olive Tapenade .................................. 30
    Sun Dried Tomato and Olive Tapenade ............ 31
    Spinach Dip with Feta, Lemon, and Oregano ..... 31
    Feta-Mint Dip with Yogurt ...................... 33
    Smoked Salmon Mousse ........................... 34
        Jan's Gougeres ............................. 35

    Meatballs in Tomato Garlic Sauce ...................... 36
    Portobello Mushrooms with Goat Cheese .......... 38
    Fried Calamari fra Diablo ................................... 39
Bread & Grains ............................................................ 41
    European Style White Bread ............................... 41
    Sour Dough Bread .............................................. 43
    White Mountain Pancakes .................................. 44
    Corn Cakes and Oat Cakes ................................. 45
        Note on Stirring Pancakes ......................... 45
    Waffles ................................................................ 46
    Polenta with Basil, Tomato & Cheese ................ 46
    White Mountain Cornbread ................................ 47
    Oatmeal Orange-Sweet Potato Bread ................. 50
    Hushpuppies ........................................................ 50
    Portuguese Style Cornbread ................................ 52
Dressings & Salads ..................................................... 55
    Grilled Antipasti ................................................. 55
        Roasting Peppers ....................................... 57
    Blue cheese dressing ........................................... 58
    Thousand Island Dressing ................................... 58
    Ranch Dressing ................................................... 58
    Café on the Common Vinaigrette ....................... 59
    Blue Cheese Vinaigrette ..................................... 59
    Lemon Basil Vinaigrette ..................................... 60
    Green Peppercorn Vinaigrette ............................ 61
    Dijon Vinaigrette ................................................ 61
    Mango Chutney ................................................... 61
    Spinach Salad with Warm Bacon Dressing ........ 62
    Spinach Salad with Raspberry Dressing ............. 63
        Candied Slivered Almonds: ....................... 64
    Maple Candied Walnuts ...................................... 65
    Spinach Salad with Oranges and Warm Goat
    Cheese ................................................................ 65
    White Mountain Salad with Creole
    Mayonnaise Dressing ......................................... 66
        Bread Croutons: ......................................... 68

- Curried Corn Salad ............................................. 69
- Soups, Stews and Chili............................................. 70
  - Grampy Ron's Chili............................................. 70
  - BearBait Chili for Jerry ....................................... 71
  - Beef Stew........................................................... 72
  - Smoked Turkey and Bean Soup ........................ 73
  - Roasted Sweet Potato and Cabbage Soup .......... 74
  - Roast Squash and Sweet Potato Soup................. 76
  - Roast Squash and Parsnip Soup......................... 77
  - Roast Squash & Yellow Tomato Soup ............... 78
  - Avocado Gazpacho............................................. 80
  - Lentil Soup with Ham and Potatoes .................... 80
  - Roasted Beet Soup.............................................. 82
  - Carrot Top Soup ................................................. 84
- Fish & Seafood.......................................................... 85
  - Fish Cakes........................................................... 85
  - Crab Cakes with Curry Sauce............................. 86
    - Curry Sauce................................................. 87
  - White Mountains Seafood Chowder................... 88
  - Trout Almandine................................................. 89
  - Beer Battered Shrimp ......................................... 91
  - Beer Batter Coconut Shrimp............................... 91
  - Beer Batter Onion Rings..................................... 92
    - Beer Batter: ................................................. 92
    - Tempura Batter............................................ 93
    - Notes on Shrimp.......................................... 93
  - Garlic Shrimp ..................................................... 96
  - Grilled Garlic Marinated Shrimp with Corn and Onion Relish................................................. 97
  - Fried White Anchovies with an Andalusian Pepper.................................................................. 99
  - Salmon with Butter-Tarragon-Mustard Sauce.. 101
  - Boiled Lobster .................................................. 102
  - Lobster Bisque.................................................. 103
  - Lobster Cakes ................................................... 104
  - Spicy Tuna Tartare ........................................... 105

Dipping Sauce ....................................................... 105
Fried Calamari ...................................................... 106
    Variation – Fried Calamari 2 ..................... 107
Calamari Cacciatore ............................................. 107
Meat ............................................................................. 109
    Cooking Meat ............................................. 109
    What Happens to Meat as It Rests? .......... 110
Lamb Provencal .................................................... 112
Grilled Center Cut Lamb Chops ......................... 113
Rack of Lamb with Stilton Crust ....................... 114
Rack of Lamb with Cardamom and Cumin ...... 115
    Cumin and Coriander variation ................ 115
Lamb Shanks a la' Carol ..................................... 116
Beef Tenderloin .................................................... 117
    Red Wine and Wild Mushroom Sauce ..... 118
Pork Tenderloin New Orleans ............................ 119
    Asian Variation .......................................... 120
    Bronk Variation ......................................... 120
    Note On Cooking Pork .............................. 120
    Southern Comfort – Maple Syrup BBQ
Sauce ................................................................ 121
Tourtiere ................................................................ 122
    Pastry Crust ................................................ 123
Veal Scaloppini and Artichoke Involtini .......... 124
Osso Bucco Ragu ................................................. 125
    Maple Ham Glaze ...................................... 127
Poultry ........................................................................ 129
Herb Roasted Chicken ......................................... 129
Chicken Piccata .................................................... 130
Chicken Salad with Roasted Red Peppers ........ 132
Chicken Curry ...................................................... 133
Duck Yellow Curry .............................................. 134
Roast Brined Duck ............................................... 136
    Why Brining Works .................................. 137
White Mountain Chicken in Wine ..................... 138

Chicken with Tortellini and Sun Dried Tomato
Pesto .................................................................. 139
Poulet a la Crème avec Jerez ........................... 141
Chicken Pot Pie ................................................ 142
Apricot Ginger Glazed Chicken with Chipotle
Sweet and Red Bliss Potatoes ........................ 144
Pasta ........................................................................ 146
Basic Tomato Sauce ......................................... 146
Pasta Dough...................................................... 147
Lobster Ravioli ................................................. 150
Grampy Ron's Mac & Cheese.......................... 151
Elicoidali with mushroom sauce....................... 153
Tortellini variation............................................ 154
Grilled Vegetable Lasagna with Puttanesca
Sauce and Pesto................................................ 154
    Puttanesca Sauce:....................................... 155
Vegetables................................................................ 157
Sweet Potato and Parsnip Hash ........................ 157
Mashed Sweet Potatoes .................................... 158
Grilled Vegetables ............................................ 158
Sweet Corn with Fennel ................................... 159
Sautéed Kale with Onion and Garlic ................ 160
    Spinach and Beet Green Variations .......... 160
Eggplant Stew................................................... 161
Deep Fried Fennel and Onions ......................... 162
Red Onion Confit.............................................. 163
Patatas Catalan.................................................. 164
Onion Chutney.................................................. 165
Grape Varieties and the Wines They Produce ........ 166
White Grapes: ................................................... 166
Red Grapes: ...................................................... 167
Index......................................................................... 169

# Conversions

| TEASPOONS | TABLE SPOONS | CUPS | FLUID OUNCES | MILLI LITERS | OTHER |
|---|---|---|---|---|---|
| 1/4 tsp | | | | 1 ml | |
| 1/2 tsp | | | | 2 ml | |
| 3/4 tsp | 1/4 Tbl | | | 4 ml | |
| 1 tsp | 1/3 Tbl | | | 5 ml | |
| 3 tsps | 1 Tbl | 1/16 c | 1/2 oz | 15 ml | |
| 6 tsps | 2 Tbls | 1/8 c | 1 oz | 30 ml | |
| | | | 1 1/2 oz | 44 ml | 1 jigger |
| 12 tsps | 4 Tbls | 1/4 c | 2 oz | 60 ml | |
| 16 tsps | 5 1/3 Tbls | 1/3 c | 2 1/2 oz | 75 ml | |
| 18 tsps | 6 Tbls | 3/8 c | 3 oz | 90 ml | |
| 24 tsps | 8 Tbls | 1/2 c | 4 oz | 125 ml | 1/4 pint |
| 32 tsps | 10 2/3 Tbls | 2/3 c | 5 oz | 150 ml | |
| 36 tsps | 12 Tbls | 3/4 c | 6 oz | 175 ml | |
| 48 tsps | 16 Tbls | 1 c | 8 oz | 237 ml | 1/2 pint |
| | | 1 1/2 cs | 12 oz | 355 ml | |
| | | 2 cs | 16 oz | 473 ml | 1 pint |
| | | 3 cs | 24 oz | 710 ml | 1 1/2 pints |
| | | | 25.6 oz | 757 ml | 1 fifth |
| | | 4 cs | 32 oz | 946 ml | 1 quart or 1 liter |
| | | 8 cs | 64 oz | | 2 quarts |
| | | 16 cs | 128 oz | | 1 gallon |

| Degrees (approximate) | | | | | | | | | |
|---|---|---|---|---|---|---|---|---|---|
| F | 200 | 250 | 300 | 325 | 350 | 375 | 400 | 425 | 450 |
| C | 100 | 120 | 150 | 160 | 175 | 190 | 200 | 220 | 230 |

# Introduction:

## *Preface by Ronald Collins*

This book is a collection of recipes created in the kitchen of the Lakes Region Culinary Institute. These recipes, like all recipes, are not created out of thin air. You will detect influences from Europe especially the Mediterranean region. The Institute is located in the southern foothills of the White Mountains in New Hampshire which has a large and vibrant Canadian French derived population, and many of the local White Mountain recipes demonstrate the wonderful influence of the French ancestors of today's northern New Hampshire people. Where appropriate the wines we serve at the Institute with each recipe are given.

Many people have contributed to my culinary experience, and therefore, to this collection. Not the least of these people have been Janice Collins, my wife, whose insights often result in a good recipe becoming a great recipe, William Bronk, an old friend who over forty years ago taught me to cook and taste, my mother who let me "cook" at the very young age of eleven, and my father who gallantly ate my many experiments from those early days.

Finally, the twenty-five years I spent traveling around the world, and my three years of living in Europe, gave me a range of culinary pleasures that have left their impressions in this collection. Every recipe in this book is a dish I serve at my own table; none are included here just for filler or show. I also served many these dishes at our restaurant, The Café on the Common and at our cooking school, the Lakes Region Culinary Institute.

During a serving of our roast brined duck at the Café on the Common, one man was so impressed he got down on one knee and proposed to his girlfriend right at the table. She accepted. That's the sign of a good duck!!

You will notice that there are no dessert recipes included. My wife, Jan, is the family dessert maker, and she deserves a book of her own. I rarely create desserts, and so I have not included any in this collection.

I hope you enjoy these dishes as much as I have. As Bronk would say after we had created together in the kitchen...

**eat, eat, enjoy, enjoy...**


## *Lakes Region Culinary Institute*

The mission and purpose of the Lakes Region Culinary Institute, located at 162 South Mayhew Turnpike in Hebron, New Hampshire, is to teach the culinary arts, develop recipes and develop cooking techniques. www.LakesRegionCulinary.com

**Note:** Throughout this book we refer to Zinfandel wine. By this we mean the full bodied red Zinfandel and not the wine called "white" Zinfandel.

**Many thanks to
Nancy Fabbri, proofreader extraordinaire.**

# Appetizers

Appetizers are an opportunity to be very creative. In every land a small well flavored little dish is a favorite. In some places they, after many courses, form the meal.

Popular throughout Spain in bars and restaurants, tapas are appetizers that usually accompany sherry or other aperitifs and cocktails. They can also form an entire meal and range from simple items such as olives or cubes of ham and cheese to more elaborate preparations like cold omelets, snails in a spicy sauce, stuffed peppers, and miniature sandwiches.

Ideal for a celebratory meal, tapas have become trendy in many American cities although it is not necessary to dine out when craving these bite-sized eats. Just gather some friends, open some sherry or a good Rioja, and serve some of Spain's tastiest treats. The best part is, you can use the saucers from your tea or coffee mugs as plates, and encourage your guests to use toothpicks or their fingers when eating as is the tradition in Spain – no silverware necessary - which means you won't have to spend hours doing the dishes!

We have included many tapas and other apps from our traveling experience.

## *Roasted Peppers with Prosciutto and Fontina*

- ✓ 3 large red bell peppers
- ✓ salt
- ✓ pepper
- ✓ 2-1/2 ounces Prosciutto
- ✓ 4-1/2 ounces imported Italian Fontina in 6 slices
- ✓ 3 tablespoons olive oil

Serves 6
Wine: a light crisp cold white wine like Pinot Grigio or Sauvignon Blanc

- Set peppers on outdoor grill, under broiler, or directly on a gas burner.
- Watch them closely and when the skin blackens turn the peppers with tongs until the entire surface is black.
- Place in a brown paper bag and close.
- After the peppers have cooled, scrape away the blackened skin with a paring knife.
- Cut the peppers in half, remove the seed and membrane.
- Lay the pepper halves out on a board, skinned side down.
- Lightly salt and pepper the insides.
- Put half a slice of Prosciutto and a slice of Fontina on each pepper.
- Fold in half and secure with a toothpick.

- Oil a shallow baking dish with 1/2 tablespoon of the oil.
- Set the peppers in the dish and drizzle the rest of the oil on top.
- Put them into a preheated 400°F oven and bake until the Fontina melts, about 10 minutes.
- Let cool briefly and remove toothpicks before serving.

## *Cherry Tomatoes Stuffed with Spanish Olive Tapenade*

For the tapenade:
- 1/2 cup Spanish olives with pimento
- 1 1/2 teaspoons drained capers
- 1 teaspoon brandy, preferably a Spanish brandy such as Solera Gran Reserva, or Fundador
- 1/4 teaspoon freshly grated lemon zest
- 2 tablespoons extra-virgin olive oil
- 32 small cherry tomatoes
- Chopped fresh parsley for garnish

Serves 8
Wine: any red wine

- Make the tapenade: in a food processor, pulse the olives until chopped fine.
- Add the remaining tapenade ingredients and pulse until olives are minced.

- With a sharp knife, slice the stem end (1/4-inch down) and the bottom (1/8-inch up) from each tomato and discard.
- Using a 1/4 teaspoon, remove the juice and seeds from each tomato half, leaving the outside shell intact.
- Spoon a generous 1/4 teaspoon of the tapenade into each shell and garnish with the parsley.

## *Blue Cheese & Walnut Coated Cherry Tomatoes*

- ✓ 2/3 cup finely chopped walnuts
- ✓ 6 ounces crumbled Cabrales (Spanish blue cheese), Blue , Roquefort or Gorgonzola may be substituted
- ✓ 4 ounces cream cheese
- ✓ 20 cherry or grape tomatoes

Serves 8
Wine: Cabernet Sauvignon or a Zinfandel

- Preheat oven to 325°F.
- On a sheet pan spread out the walnuts and toast in the oven for 7 to 9 minutes.
- Remove from oven and allow to cool.
- In a bowl with an electric mixer, cream together the blue cheese and the cream cheese until smooth.
- Put one tablespoon of the cheese mixture in the palm of one hand and in it roll a tomato, shaping the mixture around the tomato to coat.

- Cover the remaining tomatoes and chill on a sheet pan for 15 minutes.
- Roll the cheese-coated tomatoes in the walnut mixture to cover completely and chill for 30 minutes or until coating is firm.
- cut tomatoes into halves u sing a sharp knife.

Variation: Substitute Grapes for Cherry Tomatoes

## *Mushroom Puffs*

- ✓ 1 - 8 inch by 8 inch sheet of Puff Pastry
- ✓ 10 to 12 ounces of Crimi or Baby Bella Mushrooms sliced or chopped.
- ✓ 4 ounces unsalted butter.
- ✓ 1 cup chopped sweet onion
- ✓ 1 small crushed clove of garlic
- ✓ 1 tablespoon of dry Tarragon
- ✓ 1 cup of a dry white wine
- ✓ 2 tablespoons of sour cream
- ✓ 2 tablespoons grated Parmigiano Reggiano
- ✓ 1/2 teaspoon of both salt and freshly ground pepper.
- ✓ 1 egg lightly beaten

Serves 6
Wine: Pinot Noir or Merlot

- Preheat your oven to $350°F$.

- Cut the Puff pastry into 36 pieces. Arrange on a cookie pan and brush with the egg.
- Bake pastry for 8 to 10 minutes until lightly golden brown.
- Set aside and let cool.
- In a medium hot pan brown the mushrooms uncovered in 3 ounces of the butter the salt and the pepper until golden. Remove from heat and place in food processor.
- Add last ounce of butter to the same pan and add the onions and garlic and cook until the onions are translucent.
- Add the wine to the pan and cook until the wine is nearly all gone.
- Add the onion and garlic to the food processor.
- Add the tarragon, Parmigiano and sour cream to the food processor.
- Process until chopped but not too long. Do not over process or the mixture will liquefy.

To serve: cut each puff into two halves, upper and lower. Place a scant teaspoon of the mushroom mixture onto each puff lower half and cover with the puff upper half. Seal the edges. Return to a 350°F oven for 7 minutes. Serve.

## *Shrimp Mozambique*
- ✓ 2 lbs extra large or jumbo shrimp
- ✓ 1 bottle Chardonnay wine
- ✓ 1 tablespoons kosher salt

- ✓ Red pepper flakes to taste
- ✓ ¼ cup olive oil
- ✓ 8 cloves of garlic minced
- ✓ 4 tablespoons Sazon Goya con Culantro y Achiote (This Portuguese spice mix is sold in most supermarkets in the international section).
- ✓ Crusty Portuguese bread

Serves 8 as an appetizer
Wine: Chardonnay or Vouvray

- In a deep stove top pot sauté garlic and shrimp until shrimp are done.
- Add Sazon Goya, salt and red pepper flakes and mix well
- Add wine and bring to a boil
- Cook for 2 minutes

Serve in soup bowls and large chunks of bread on the side to soak up the wonderful salty, spicy juices.

## *Blue Cheese Shortbreads with Walnuts and Chutney*

- ✓ 1/2 cup crumbled blue cheese or gorgonzola
- ✓ 3 ounces unsalted butter
- ✓ 1/2 cup chopped walnuts
- ✓ 1/2 cup all purpose flour
- ✓ 1/4 cup corn starch
- ✓ 1/2 teaspoon each salt & pepper
- ✓ 6 ounces cream cheese (whipped cream cheese works as well)

- ✓ 6 ounces mango chutney or onion chutney (recipes in this book)
- ✓ Fresh parsley leaves for garnish
- ✓ Walnut halves for garnish.

Serves 6
Wine: Vouvray or Gewurztraminer

- In a food processor add the blue cheese, butter and chopped walnuts. Process until smooth.
- Add the flour, cornstarch, salt and pepper. Process only until mixed.
- The mix will appear dry, but remove it from the processor and form into a ball. The cheese and butter will bind everything together.
- Wrap the dough ball in plastic wrap and set in the refrigerator for 30 minutes.
- Preheat oven to 350°F.
- After 30 minutes remove dough from the refrigerator and place between the sheets of plastic wrap.
- Roll out dough until about 1/8 inch thick
- Use a cookie cutter about 1.5 to 2 inches across to cut out 18 or so pieces of the shortbread dough.
- Bake shortbread dough on a cookie sheet for about 20 to 25 minutes until just a light brown. If you overcook the shortbreads they will taste awful so keep an eye on them.

After baking let them cool, and then spread a teaspoon of cream cheese, and a dab of chutney on each one and then top with a walnut and a leaf of parsley.

## *Shrimp Scampi Quesadillas*

- ✓ 4 burrito size tortilla wrappers
- ✓ 1 pound large cooked shrimp
- ✓ 3 cloves garlic minced
- ✓ 2 tablespoons of olive oil
- ✓ 1 teaspoon oregano or marjoram
- ✓ 1 lb shredded Monterey Jack or Mozzarella cheese

Each pair of tortilla wrappers Serves 2
Wine: a light bodied red like Pinot Noir or a heavy white like Chardonnay

- Pre-heat oven to 425°F
- On a tortilla wrapper arrange 12 – 16 shrimp depending upon size
- Sprinkle 1 tablespoon of minced garlic over shrimp
- Sprinkle 1 teaspoon oregano over shrimp
- Add ½ lb of Monterey Jack to cover shrimp
- On top place another tortilla wrapper
- Brush top with olive oil
- On cookie sheet bake for 5-7 minutes until top wrapper begins to toast.
- Slice and serve.

## *Rosemary and Parmesan Savories*

- ✓ 4 tablespoons unsalted butter
- ✓ 2 tablespoons chopped fresh rosemary
- ✓ 3 tablespoons grated Parmigiano-Reggiano
- ✓ 2 sheets of puff pastry
- ✓ Kosher Salt

Serves eight
Wine: any dry white or red wine

- Pre-heated oven to 425°F
- Rollout pastry sheets
- Coat both pastry sheets with the butter
- Sprinkle ½ on the Parmesan cheese evenly onto sheets
- Sprinkle rosemary evenly over sheets
- Roll two edges of each sheet toward the center
- Wrap each sheet in plastic and chill for at least one hour
- When ready to finish, slice each rolled up sheet into about 20 slices.
- Arrange on a cookie sheet and sprinkle with remaining Parmesan cheese and salt
- Bake until golden brown, about 4 minutes

## Grilled Vegetable Pita Pizzas with Sun Dried Tomato Pesto

- 1 eggplant
- 1 large sweet onion
- 1 red pepper roasted (see Grilled Antipasti recipe)
- 1 yellow pepper roasted
- 4 Portabella Mushrooms
- 8 ounces sun dried tomato pesto (recipe is below)
- 4 ounces grated Parmigiano-Reggiano cheese
- 4 large pita breads
- 2 tablespoons of olive oil
- garlic
- salt & pepper

Serves: 8 to 10
Wine: Merlot or Rioja

- Cut roasted peppers into strips, sprinkle with olive oil and crushed garlic. Let marinate while the rest of the preparation is being done.
- Slice the eggplant lengthwise into ¼ inch thick slices.
- Slice the onion into ¼ thick slices.
- Brush one side of the mushrooms, eggplant slices and onion slices with olive oil and sprinkle with salt and pepper.

- Grill or broil mushrooms, eggplant and onions over medium high heat with oiled side toward the heat.
- Grill or broil the eggplant for 3 to 4 minutes per side.
- Grill or broil the mushrooms and onions for 5 to 6 minutes per side or until done.
- Note: Turn them over only once during the broiling or grilling and brush with olive oil, and sprinkle with salt and pepper after turning. As grills and broilers vary, keep a close eye on the vegetables and turn when you see a good color develop.
- Slice mushrooms into strips.
- If you grilled the vegetables then heat the broiler for the last step.
- Onto to each pita spread 2 ounces of sun dried tomato pesto
- Sprinkle 1 ounce of the parmesan cheese onto each pita.
- Arrange the vegetables onto the pitas in any pattern that suits you.
- Brush each pita lightly with olive oil
- Broil until the edges of the pita begins to turn brown.
- Slice into wedges and serve.

## Sun Dried Tomato Pesto

- ✓ 1 cup of sun dried tomatoes
- ✓ ½ cup of olive oil. If your sun dried tomatoes came packed in oil then use that.

- ✓ 2 cloves of garlic
- ✓ 2 ounces grated parmesan cheese
- ✓ 1 tablespoon of capers

- Place all ingredients into a food processor
- Process until chopped into a fine, but not pureed, paste.
- If the paste is too thick add more olive oil.

## Note on Parmesan Cheese

While it will cost you a little bit more, Parmigiano-Reggiano has a depth and complexity of flavor and a smooth, melting texture that none of the domestic or other imported parmesan cheeses can match.

Parmigiano-Reggiano owes much of its flavor to the unpasteurized milk used to produce it. It is a "controlled-district" cheese, which means not only that it must be made within the boundaries of this zone but also that the milk used to make it and even the grass, hay, and grain fed to the cows that make the milk must come from the district. Consequently, "Just like good wine, a lot of character comes from its soil and climate."

The low salt content of Parmigiano-Reggiano makes it more perishable than other cheeses once cut from the wheel. Once cut, the cheese will also begin to dry out. This was evident in the Parmigiano-Reggiano sample purchased at the grocery store. Tasters rated this a few tenths of a point lower than the sample purchased at the specialty cheese store because of a chalky finish. This drying effect was even more glaring with chalky pre-grated products, which.

Another benefit of the larger wheel is that Parmigiano-Reggiano can age longer. Parmigiano-Reggiano ages for about 24 months, while domestic Parmesan ages for about 10 months. The longer aging allows more complex flavors and aromas to develop. The aging also makes a difference in texture, creating a distinctive component that tasters described as "crystal crunch." The crunch stems from proteins breaking down into free amino acid crystals during the latter half of the aging process. The crystals are visible, appearing as white dots in the cheese. No other Parmesan has this effect.

Other textural differences are created by the fact that the curds for Parmigiano-Reggiano are cut into fragments the size of wheat grains, which are much finer than the fragments created in the manufacture of domestic Parmesan. The benefit of smaller curds is that they drain more effectively. Domestic Parmesans have to be mechanically pressed to get rid of excess moisture. The consequence is a cheese that is much more dense: it can be characterized as "rubbery," "tough," and "squeaky".

That is not say that all of the other Parmesans are completely unacceptable-just most. One domestic parmesan to be recommended is Wisconsin-made DiGiorno. So while there are more affordable Parmesan options, the Parmigiano-Reggiano is in a class of its own. When added to a dish it acts as more than a seasoning; it can add a complex spectrum of flavor. And, as I found, Italians commonly eat Parmigiano-Reggiano in chunks as a table food; it makes for a tempting snack while preparing a complementary meal.

## *Roast Beef & Gorgonzola Salad*

This recipe comes from good friend and neighbor Carol LaFontaine. Carol is the salad queen. She invents and adapts and creates some of the best salads I've had. It seems to be an enviable natural talent for her. Use this salad as a side dish or serve as an appetizer on cocktail size breads and/or crackers.

- ✓ 1 ½ lb Rare, thinly sliced roast beef, cut into shreds and pieces
- ✓ 6 to 8 ounces of Gorgonzola, Blue Cheese or Stilton broken into crumbles
- ✓ ½ cup chopped Walnuts
- ✓ ¾ cup Extra Virgin Olive Oil
- ✓ 2 tablespoons of red wine vinegar or sherry vinegar
- ✓ 1 tablespoon of Dijon mustard
- ✓ ¼ teaspoon each of kosher salt and ground black pepper
- ✓ 2 tablespoon of dried herbs, we recommend Herbs de Provence from Penzeys Spices

Serves 4 to 6 as a side dish
Wine: a full bodied red like a Cabernet Sauvignon or a Chianti Classico

- In a large bowl mix all ingredients until all the beef is covered with the oil, vinegar and herbs.

Note: Once you add the vinegar to the beef a chemical form of cooking starts. So, mix all of the ingredients except the beef (this makes a vinaigrette that goes very well over greens and other salad fixings). Then no more than ½ hour before serving mix the beef into the vinaigrette.

## *Asian Beef Skewers*

- ✓ 1 lb rib eye steak cut into strips 1 inch wide, ¼ inch thick and at least 4 inches long.
- ✓ 2 tablespoons of Sesame Oil
- ✓ 2 cloves of garlic minced
- ✓ 1 tablespoon of ginger grated fine
- ✓ ¼ cup soy sauce
- ✓ 2 tablespoons Thai Chili Sauce (that made by Kikkoman is fine to use)
- ✓ Bamboo or metal skewers

Serves 2

Wine: a strong red to stand to this much flavor, so we recommend an Old Vine Zinfandel or Malbec or Shiraz.

- Place all ingredients into a zip lock bag
- Mix well with your hands
- Marinate overnight in the refrigerator

- Build skewers and grill over a hot grill for 2 minutes per side.

## *Black Bean & Garlic Hummus*

This recipe actually works better with canned beans than with freshly cooked ones.

- ✓ 1 16-ounce can of black beans
- ✓ 2 tablespoons of extra virgin olive oil
- ✓ Juice from 1 medium size lemon
- ✓ 2 tablespoons of sesame tahini
- ✓ 2 tablespoons of toasted sesame oil
- ✓ ¼ to ½ teaspoon cumin powder depending upon your preference
- ✓ 2 to 3 garlic cloves depending upon your preference
- ✓ ½ teaspoon salt

Serves 4 to 6
Wine: any dry wine will do

- Drain beans but retain all juice from the bean can.
- In a food processor add all ingredients except juice from bean can.
- Blend until smooth.
- If the hummus is too thick use juice from bean can to thin until you reach a consistency you like.

Serve this with toasted pita breads. Take good quality fresh pitas and toast them directly over the flames of a gas stove for 10 to 15 seconds per side.

If you do not have a gas stove you place them under a hot broiler for 10 to 15 seconds per side.

## Note on Garlic

Raw garlic cloves contain a sulfur-based compound called alliin and an enzyme called alliinase. These two elements are not in contact in raw garlic, which is why a head of garlic has almost no aroma. When the garlic is cut, the enzyme comes into contact with the alliin and converts it to allicin, a new and very pungent compound that gives raw garlic its typical aroma. This compound also gives garlic its bite.

When you slice garlic, only a small amount of enzyme and sulfur compound come into contact, so just a small amount of allicin is produced. The result is a mild garlic flavor. When you mince garlic, however, more allicin is produced because there's more contact between the sulfur compound and the enzyme. More allicin means more aroma and flavor.

For the strongest garlic flavor, put the cloves through a press or mince them into a smooth paste. Chopped (as opposed to minced) garlic has a moderate amount of flavor and aroma, while sliced garlic has the least. Because heat breaks down the harsh-tasting allicin, roasting or toasting garlic cloves before adding them to a dish will pretty much eliminate any harsh garlic flavor. If you want a strong garlic flavor, add it to your recipe late in the process. The later the more garlic flavor.

## Note: What about the Green Shoots That Sometimes Sprout From Garlic?

Many a cook has been told to remove any green shoots from cloves of garlic because they are thought to have a bitter taste that persists even when the garlic is cooked. A test was made using raw garlic in aioli and cooked garlic in pasta with olive oil and tried each recipe with the shoots removed before mincing the garlic as well as with the shoots left in. The results: the aioli had a more bitter, unpleasant taste in the batch made with the shoots left in; the batch without the shoots still had the bite that you expect from garlic, but it was less harsh. The pasta made with the shoots had a harsh, somewhat metallic aftertaste that, once established, tainted every bite that followed.

According to Barbara Klein, a professor of sensory science at the University of Illinois at Urbana, the sprouts contain stronger, more bitter-tasting compounds than those found in the clove, and they tend to persist even after cooking. Klein said that when cooking she always removes the sprouts, and we recommend this practice.

## Note on Black Olives

Prized in Provence for their nutty, smoky flavor, tiny black Niçoise olives are a staple of the region's cuisine and the traditional olive of choice for topping a pissaladière. These brine-cured olives are generally sold loose or packed in deli containers, and they cost a pretty penny, usually $11 per pound or more (and most of that weight is pit!).

Canned black "California" olives are really green olives colored black with a chemical additive and should not be used for any purpose.

Greek kalamata olives, both fresh and jarred, are briny and fruity. They really cannot stand in for the Niçoise in recipes calling for Niçoise, but are wonderful in their own right.

Salt-cured black olives, sometimes erroneously labeled "oil-cured", and known for their wrinkled exterior, are very salty and bitter so use carefully.

We do not use the oversized cerignola, which are so mild that their use in recipes results in almost no olive flavor at all.

For a truly authentic black olive, seek out real Niçoise olives or save a few bucks and go with the common kalamata -- odds are you won't know the difference.

Best Choice: Niçoise - "Smoky" and "nutty".

Best Pinch Hitter: Kalamata - "Fruity," and "briny".

Too Overpowering: Salt Cured - "Harsh," "bitter," and "salty."

Too Meek: Cerignola - "Bland" and "mild."

Unacceptable for any use: California "Black Olives".

## *Olive Tapenade*
- ✓ 1 cup mix of pitted Niçoise olives and pitted Kalamata olives
- ✓ 2 small cloves garlic
- ✓ 2 teaspoon lemon juice
- ✓ 1 shallot, peeled and chopped

- ✓ 2 tablespoons capers
- ✓ 3 anchovy fillets, optional
- ✓ Kosher salt and black pepper
- ✓ 1/4 cup extra-virgin olive oil

Serves 4 to 6

- Place all ingredients in food processor and chop until consistency of sweet relish.
- Serve with grilled pitas, or crackers or use as a spread for sandwiches.

## *Sun Dried Tomato and Olive Tapenade*

Add ¼ cup of sun dried tomatoes to the recipe above. You may need to increase amount of olive oil a little.

## *Spinach Dip with Feta, Lemon, and Oregano*

Frozen spinach works best for this recipe. Partial thawing of the spinach produces a cold dip that can be served without further chilling. If you don't own a microwave, the frozen spinach can be thawed at room temperature for 1-1/2 hours then squeezed of excess liquid. The garlic must be minced or pressed before going into the food processor; otherwise the dip will contain large chunks of garlic.

- ✓ 1 - 10 ounces package of frozen spinach, well drained
- ✓ 1/2 cup sour cream
- ✓ 1/2 cup mayonnaise
- ✓ 2 tablespoons thin-sliced scallions white parts only, from 3 medium scallions
- ✓ 1 tablespoon fresh dill, chopped
- ✓ 1/2 cup fresh parsley, packed
- ✓ 1 small clove of garlic, minced or pressed through garlic press (about 1 teaspoon)
- ✓ 1/4 teaspoon ground black pepper
- ✓ 2 tablespoons fresh oregano or 1 tablespoon of dried Turkish Oregano
- ✓ 2 ounces feta cheese, crumbled (about 1/2 cup)
- ✓ 1 tablespoon lemon juice
- ✓ 1 teaspoon lemon zest, grated

Serves 6-10
Wine: Pinot Grigio chilled

- Thaw spinach in microwave for 3 minutes at 40 percent power. (Edges should be thawed but not warm; center should be soft enough to be broken apart into icy chunks.) Squeeze partially frozen spinach of excess water.
- In food processor, process spinach, sour cream, mayonnaise, dills, scallions, parsley, garlic, pepper, oregano, feta cheese, lemon juice, and lemon zest until smooth and creamy, about 30 seconds. Transfer mixture to

medium bowl and adjust seasoning with salt; serve.

Note: Dip can be covered with plastic wrap and refrigerated up to 2 days.

## *Feta-Mint Dip with Yogurt*

- ✓ 1/2 cup mayonnaise
- ✓ 2 1/2 ounces feta cheese , crumbled (1/2 cup)
- ✓ 1/4 cup fresh mint , chopped
- ✓ 2 medium scallions , roughly chopped
- ✓ 2 teaspoons lemon juice from 1 lemon

Serves 2-4
Wine: Vouvray

- Place yogurt in fine-mesh strainer or cheesecloth-lined colander set over bowl. Cover with plastic wrap and refrigerate 8 to 24 hours; discard liquid in bowl.
- Process all ingredients in food processor until smooth and creamy, about 30 seconds. Transfer dip to serving bowl, cover with plastic wrap, and refrigerate until flavors are blended, at least 1 hour; serve cold with crudités. (Can be refrigerated in airtight container for up to 2 days.)

Serve with grilled pitas

## *Smoked Salmon Mousse*
- 4 ounces smoked salmon (use trimmings and left over pieces)
- 16 ounces Cream Cheese
- 1 tablespoon heavy cream
- Dash Cayenne Pepper
- 1 teaspoon fresh lemon juice
- salt to taste

Serves 4 to 6
Wine: Chardonnay

- Bring cream cheese to near room temperature.
- Add all ingredients to food processor and blend until smooth.
- Serve as a dip or spread for crackers, as a stuffing for gougeres (recipe below), or a stuffing for celery.

## Jan's Gougeres

- 1 cup water
- 1/2 cup (1 stick) unsalted butter, cut into small pieces
- 1/2 teaspoon salt
- 1 cup all-purpose flour
- 4 to 5 large eggs
- 1 1/2 cups coarsely grated Gruyere

Makes 24
Wine: any wine you like

- Preheat oven to 375°F. Lightly grease 2 baking sheets or line with parchment paper.
- In a heavy saucepan bring water to a boil with butter and salt over high heat and reduce heat to moderate. Add flour all at once and beat with a wooden spoon until mixture pulls away from side of pan.
- Transfer mixture to a bowl and with an electric mixer on high-speed beat in 4 eggs, 1 at a time, beating well after each addition. Batter should be stiff enough to just hold soft peaks and fall softly from a spoon. If batter is too stiff, in a small bowl beat remaining egg lightly and add to batter a little at a time, beating on high speed, until batter is desired consistency. This batter is called Pate a Choux.

- Stir Gruyere into pate a choux and arrange level tablespoons about 1-inch apart on baking sheets. Bake in upper and lower thirds of oven, switching position of sheets halfway through baking, 30 minutes, or until puffed, golden, and crisp.
- Gougeres keep, chilled in sealable plastic bags 2 days or frozen 1 week. Reheat gougeres, uncovered in a preheated 350°F oven 10 minutes if chilled or 15 minutes if unthawed frozen.

## *Meatballs in Tomato Garlic Sauce*

Meatballs:
- ✓ 1 large onion, chopped fine
- ✓ 1 large green bell pepper, chopped fine
- ✓ 1/4 cup plus 2 tablespoons olive oil
- ✓ 2 pounds ground beef (not lean)
- ✓ 1/2 pound ground pork (not lean)
- ✓ 2/3 cup fine dry bread crumbs
- ✓ 2 1/2 teaspoons salt
- ✓ 1/4 teaspoon freshly grated nutmeg
- ✓ 1/4 cup minced fresh parsley leaves

Sauce:
- ✓ 4 large garlic cloves, minced
- ✓ 1 tablespoon olive oil
- ✓ 1 (33 1/2-ounce) can whole tomatoes, including juice
- ✓ 3/4 teaspoon dried oregano, crumbled

Serves 8 to 10
Wine: Chianti Classico or Barolo

**Meatballs**
- In a 9-inch heavy well-seasoned skillet cook onion and bell pepper in 2 tablespoons oil over moderately low heat, stirring occasionally, until softened.
- Cool mixture.
- In a large bowl combine well onion mixture, ground meat, bread crumbs, salt, nutmeg, and parsley.
- Form level tablespoons of mixture into balls (about 90).
- In skillet heat 1 tablespoon oil over moderately high heat until hot but not smoking and brown meatballs in batches (about 16 at a time), shaking skillet frequently so that meatballs maintain their shape and adding remaining 3 tablespoons oil as necessary.
- Transfer meatballs with a slotted spoon as browned to a bowl.

**Sauce:**
- In a heavy kettle (at least 6 quarts) cook garlic in oil over moderately low heat, stirring, until fragrant, about 15 seconds.
- Add tomatoes with juice and oregano and simmer, breaking up tomatoes.

- Add meatballs and simmer, covered, gently stirring occasionally, 25 minutes, or until meatballs are tender and sauce is thickened slightly.
- Transfer meatballs with slotted spoon to heated serving dish.
- If sauce seems thin, boil gently, stirring frequently, until thickened to desired consistency.
- Season sauce with salt and pepper and spoon over meatballs.

Meatballs and sauce may be made 2 days ahead. Let it cool uncovered and chill covered. reheat meatballs before serving.

## *Portobello Mushrooms with Goat Cheese*

- ✓ 2 large tomatoes, cut in half and seeds removed
- ✓ 4 medium Portobello mushrooms, cleaned and stem trimmed
- ✓ 1 goat cheese log, sliced into 4 rounds and edges rolled in crushed peppercorns
- ✓ 1 tablespoon maple syrup
- ✓ 1 tablespoon red wine vinegar
- ✓ 1 teaspoon salt
- ✓ 1 teaspoon pepper
- ✓ 1 teaspoon Dijon mustard
- ✓ ½ cup extra virgin olive oil

Serves: 2
Wine: Pinot Noir or Beaujolais

- Mix maple syrup, red wine vinegar, salt, pepper, mustard and olive oil into a tight contained and shake to mix. This will be the dressing.
- Place tomatoes and Portobellos in a plastic resealable bag or covered container.
- Pour dressing over tomatoes and mushrooms enough to coat. Allow to set at least 2 hours.
- Preheat oven to 350°F.
- Put Portobellos in a baking pan with some of the dressing used for marinade.
- Bake mushrooms in oven, covered with foil - 45 minutes to an hour.
- During the last 15 minutes of baking time, put tomato halves in pan to bake.
- To assemble layers, start with the Portobello mushroom, stem side up.
- Follow with a tomato half, and then top with a goat cheese round.

## *Fried Calamari fra Diablo*

- ✓ 1 lb Calamari cut into rings about ¼ inch thick
- ✓ 1 cup flour
- ✓ ¼ cup of Cajun spice or red pepper of your choice
- ✓ large deep pan with 2 inches of peanut or canola oil (make sure pan is deep enough that the oil docs not come more than halfway up the inside of the pan. When in doubt use a deeper pan.)

✓ Salt to taste.

Serves 3 to 4 as an appetizer
Wine: Merlot or Zinfandel

- Heat oil to 350°F.
- In a large plastic bag or storage bag combine flour and Cajun spice or /red pepper.
- Slice your Calamari into rings about ¼ inch thick.
- When all the Calamari is sliced then place all of it in the bag with the flour.
- Close the top of the bag and shake until all Calamari is coated.
- When oil reaches 350°F, shake excess flour from Calamari and gently place Calamari in the hot oil. Do this in batches small enough that the Calamari is not crowded together in the pan.
- Cook 3 to 4 minutes.
- Remove Calamari from oil, drain on paper towel and sprinkle with salt.

Continue cooking in uncrowded batches until all are done.

# Bread & Grains

## *European Style White Bread*

- ✓ 3 cups of all purpose or bread flour
- ✓ ½ cup of whole wheat flour
- ✓ 1 package yeast
- ✓ 1 tablespoon salt
- ✓ 2 tablespoons olive oil
- ✓ 1 tablespoon sugar
- ✓ 1 ½ cups of warm water

Makes 1 or 2 loaves

- Add sugar and yeast to warm water and let proof for 5 minutes.
- In large bowl and mixing machine add the flour, salt.
- After 5 minutes add the water with yeast
- Add the olive oil
- Mix well for 5 minutes. If the dough is a little dry add 1 tablespoon of water. If the dough is a little wet add ¼ cup of flour.
- Turn out onto floured work surface and knead for 5 minutes.
- Set in a large bowl and coat with olive oil
- Cover with damp cloth or plastic wrap and set in warm spot for 2 hours.
- After 2 hours turn out onto floured work surface and knead for 5 minutes.

- Divide into 2 long, French style loaves, or leave as one large Italian style loaf.
- Place on baking sheet and cover with damp cloth or plastic wrap.
- Set in warm place for 1 hour.
- Preheat oven to 375°F.
- After the 1 hour second rise place loaves slice shallow slanted cuts every 2 inches or so in the top of the loaves.
- Place in the hot oven and bake for 30 minutes if two loaves or 35 if one large loaf.

Notes:
- ❖ You can determine the crustiness of this bread by choosing different baking temperatures and by controlling the moisture in the oven: the hotter the oven, and the more moisture in the oven, the crustier the bread.
- ❖ You can add moisture by placing a pan of boiling water on the floor of the oven while baking.
- ❖ Raising the baking temperature up to as high as 425°F also gives a heartier crust but shorten the baking time by 5 minutes for every 25°F above 375°F.

## Sour Dough Bread

This is a variation on the European White Bread given on the previous page

**Day 1**
- Mix the yeast and 1 cup of the water and 1 cup of the flour.
- Cover and place in cool place, but not refrigerated, and let sit.
- This will be your sour dough starter.

**Day 2**
- Add the whole wheat flour, and salt to the starter and mix well
- Cover and place in cool place, but not refrigerated, and let sit.

**Day 3**
- Add remaining ingredients, Mix well for 5 minutes. If the dough is a little dry add 1 tablespoon of water. If the dough is a little wet add ¼ cup flour.
- Turn out onto floured work surface and knead for 5 minutes.
- Cover with damp cloth or plastic wrap and set in warm spot for 2 hours.
- After 2 hours turn out onto floured work surface and knead for 5 minutes.
- Divide into 2 long, French style loaves, or leave as one large Italian style loaf.
- Place on baking sheet and cover with damp cloth or plastic wrap.

- Set in warm place for 1 hour.
- Preheat oven to 375°F.
- After the 1 hour second rise place loaves slice shallow slanted cuts every 2 inches or so in the top of the loaves.
- Place in the hot oven and bake for 30 minutes if two loaves or 35 if one large loaf.
- If you start this bread in a 450°F oven for 15 minutes and then reduce temperature to 350°F for the remaining time you will get a real crusty bread.

## *White Mountain Pancakes*

This is my version of the pancakes served at the logging camps in the 19th century.

- ✓ 1 cup flour
- ✓ 1 cup milk
- ✓ 2 eggs
- ✓ 1 tablespoon sugar
- ✓ ½ teaspoon salt
- ✓ 1 ½ teaspoon baking powder
- ✓ 3 tablespoon melted butter

Serves 2-3

- Mix all dry ingredients
- Add eggs and milk and stir
- Add butter and stir until smooth
- Let rest 5 minutes
- Onto a well heated and oiled griddle pour 1/3 of a cup of batter for each pancake

- Cook until golden brown, about 4 minutes.
- Flip and repeat

If you want blueberry or pecan pancakes add ¾ cup of either to batter just before cooking and carefully fold in.

## Corn Cakes and Oat Cakes

We make this from left over corn grits or oatmeal

- Add ½ to 1 cup of cold cooked corn grits or oatmeal after you add the butter.
- Mix until smooth.
- Cook the same as above.

These cakes will be amazing light and fluffy.

## Note on Stirring Pancakes for Fluffiness

There are two factors that promote fluffiness in pancake batter, underdeveloped gluten and dissolved baking soda. Gluten is a mix of very long proteins that are disorganized in structure. Once gluten is dissolved in water, these proteins can more easily rearrange their structure. Kneading or mixing gluten elongates the proteins and somewhat organizes them, an action similar to combing the strands of your hair. As the proteins start to lie more or less parallel to each other, the dough becomes elastic and less tender. By reducing the mixing time of your batter, you give the gluten less opportunity to organize.

Baking soda (either on its own or as part of the baking powder formula) creates the bubbles that make pancakes rise. When baking soda encounters an acid, carbon dioxide is formed to produce the bubbles in the batter. The stirring of the pancake batter speeds bubble formation by moving the baking soda and acid together. Unfortunately, stirring also causes the release of carbon dioxide gas by bringing formed bubbles to the surface of the mixture. Just a little too much stirring and the bubble-forming capacity of the baking soda will be quickly exhausted. To make the fluffiest pancakes possible, then, you should stir the batter until the ingredients are just incorporated—and not one stir more!

## *Waffles*

To any of the recipes for pancakes above, leave out 2 tablespoons of milk and add one egg. This converts the pancake batter to a waffle batter.

## *Polenta with Basil, Tomato & Cheese*

- ✓ 2 teaspoons Extra Virgin Olive Oil
- ✓ 2 cups chopped sweet onion
- ✓ 4 cups chicken broth
- ✓ 2 cups of fresh corn kernels
- ✓ 2 cloves of garlic
- ✓ 1 cup of quick grits or instant polenta
- ✓ ½ c grated Parmigiano-Reggiano

- ½ teaspoon kosher salt
- Black pepper to taste
- 1 cup chopped deseeded tomatoes
- ½ cup chopped fresh basil

Serves eight

- Sauté Onions in the Olive Oil until tender
- Add corn and garlic and sauté for 1 minute
- Add broth, salt and pepper; and cook for 5 minutes
- Slowly add polenta and stirring continuously, cook until thick, about 5 minutes
- Add cheese and stir in
- Remove from the heat
- Keep warm until serving time. Just before serving sprinkle with tomato and basil

## *White Mountain Cornbread*

- 1 1/4 cups fine white cornmeal
- 2 teaspoons salt
- 1 1/4 cups boiling water
- 1 teaspoon granulated sugar
- 1 cup lukewarm water, divided
- 1 tablespoon active dry yeast (or 1 15 ml pkg)
- 3 cups all-purpose flour
- 1/2 cup white corn flour (approx. measure)

2 loaves   3¾ hours 3 hours prep

- In a large mixing bowl, mix the cornmeal and salt together, then add the boiling water and stir until smooth.
- Let this cool until mixture is lukewarm (should take about 10 minutes).
- Meanwhile, in a measuring cup, dissolve the sugar in 1/2 cup of the lukewarm water and sprinkle in the yeast; let stand for 10 minutes.
- Now rapidly whisk the yeast mixture with a fork and then stir into the cornmeal mixture.
- A bit at a time, mix in the all-purpose flour, stopping a few times to slowly add in the remaining 1/2 cup lukewarm water; blend this mixture well, until completely combined.
- Turn this mixture out onto a well-floured surface and knead until elastic and all ingredients are well blended; this will likely take about 10 minutes.
- If you need to -- and only if you NEED to -- add a bit more flour; you will likely need to if your kitchen is at all humid, as that can keep the dough a little sticky.
- When smooth and elastic, gather the dough into a ball.
- Lightly grease a fairly large mixing bowl and put the dough into bowl, turning dough so it is greased all over.

- Cover bowl with a clean tea towel, place in a draft-free area (try the top of your fridge, or inside your oven -- not turned on of course) and let dough rise until doubled in bulk, which should take about 90 minutes.
- Now punch down the dough and shape it into either one round loaf or two small ones; have ready a well greased baking sheet or a well greased pie plate.
- Roll the loaf (loaves) in corn flour until well covered, then, if you've made the two small loaves, place on baking sheet, or if you've prepared just the one large loaf, place on pie plate.
- Cover with clean tea towel and let rise in a draft-free place for 45 minutes, or until doubled in size.
- Brush with water or olive oil before baking.
- Place metal sheet pan in oven on lowest rack and half fill with water.
- Place a rack in oven directly above the sheet pan, and place a baking stone on this rack.
- Preheat oven to $400°F$.
- Bake bread on baking stone for 30 to 40 minutes, or until loaves sound hollow when tapped on bottom; they should be golden brown and crusty on top.
- Transfer to wire racks to cool.

## *Oatmeal Orange-Sweet Potato Bread*

- ✓ 1 ½ cups cooked oatmeal
- ✓ 2 egg yolks
- ✓ 1 small sweet potato cooked and mashed
- ✓ 2 tablespoon orange oil
- ✓ 1 tablespoons orange blossom honey
- ✓ 1 teaspoon salt
- ✓ 1 ¼ cups warm water
- ✓ 3 cups unbleached flour
- ✓ yeast

makes one loaf

- Add yeast to the water, let stand 5 minutes.
- In mixer combine flour and salt.
- Add water-yeast mix to the flour-salt mix.
- Mix at low speed.
- While mixer is running add all remaining ingredients.
- Mix for 5 minutes.
- Place mixture in greased bread loaf pan.
- Let rise until double in bulk.
- Preheat oven to 350°F.
- Bake at 350°F for 35-45 minutes.

## *Hushpuppies*

- ✓ 1 cup flour
- ✓ 1/2 cup yellow cornmeal
- ✓ 1/2 cup masa flour
- ✓ 1 tablespoon baking powder

- ✓ 2 teaspoons salt
- ✓ 1/2 cup chopped onions
- ✓ 1/2 cup chopped bell peppers
- ✓ 1 tablespoon chopped garlic
- ✓ 3 eggs, beaten
- ✓ 1 cup milk
- ✓ 1/2 cup vegetable oil
- ✓ 1/2 teaspoon
- ✓ Tabasco hot sauce
- ✓ 2 teaspoons Worcestershire sauce
- ✓ Oil for frying
- ✓ Salt and pepper

- Preheat the fryer. In a mixing bowl, combine all the dry ingredients.
- Stir in the onions, bell peppers, and garlic.
- Stir in the eggs, milk, oil, Tabasco sauce, and Worcestershire sauce.
- Mix the batter until all the ingredients are incorporated.
- Carefully spoon a tablespoon of the batter at a time into the hot oil.
- Fry the hushpuppies until golden brown, stirring constantly for overall browning, about 3 minutes.
- Remove the hushpuppies from the oil and drain on a paper-lined plate.
- Season with salt and pepper.

Yield: about 2 dozen hushpuppies

## *Portuguese Style Cornbread*

- ✓ 1 1/4 cups fine white cornmeal
- ✓ 2 teaspoons salt
- ✓ 1 1/4 cups boiling water
- ✓ 1 teaspoon granulated sugar
- ✓ 1 cup lukewarm water, divided
- ✓ 1 tablespoon active dry yeast (or 1 15-ml pkg)
- ✓ 3 cups all-purpose flour
- ✓ 1/2 cup white corn flour (approx. measure)

2 loaves   3¾ hours 3 hours prep

- In a large mixing bowl, mix the cornmeal and salt together, then add the boiling water and stir until smooth.
- Let this cool until mixture is lukewarm (should take about 10 minutes).
- Meanwhile, in a measuring cup, dissolve the sugar in 1/2 cup of the lukewarm water and sprinkle in the yeast; let stand for 10 minutes.
- Now rapidly whisk the yeast mixture with a fork and then stir into the cornmeal mixture.
- A bit at a time, mix in the all-purpose flour, stopping a few times to slowly add in the remaining 1/2 cup lukewarm water; blend this mixture well, until completely combined.
- Turn this mixture out onto a well-floured surface and knead until elastic

and all ingredients are well blended; this will likely take about 10 minutes.
- If you need to -- and only if you NEED to -- add a bit more flour; you will likely need to if your kitchen is at all humid, as that can keep the dough a little sticky.
- When smooth and elastic, gather the dough into a ball.
- Lightly grease a fairly large mixing bowl and put the dough into bowl, turning dough so it is greased all over.
- Cover bowl with a clean tea towel, place in a draft-free area (try the top of your fridge, or inside your oven -- not turned on of course) and let dough rise until doubled in bulk, which should take about 90 minutes.
- Now punch down the dough and shape it into either one round loaf or two small ones; have ready a well greased baking sheet or a well greased pie plate.
- Roll the loaf (loaves) in corn flour until well covered, then, if you've made the two small loaves, place on baking sheet, or if you've prepared just the one large loaf, place on pie plate.
- Cover with clean tea towel and let rise in a draft-free place for 45 minutes, or until doubled in size.
- Brush with water or olive oil before baking.

- Place metal sheet pan in oven on lowest rack and half fill with water.
- Place a rack in oven directly above the sheet pan, and place a baking stone on this rack.
- Preheat oven to 400°F.
- Bake bread in on baking stone for 30 to 40 minutes, or until loaves sound hollow when tapped on bottom; they should be golden brown and crusty on top.
- Transfer to wire racks to cool.

# Dressings & Salads

## *Grilled Antipasti*

- ✓ 1 lb boneless, skinned chicken breast
- ✓ 8 ounces aged provolone cheese
- ✓ 1 eggplant
- ✓ 1 large sweet onion
- ✓ 1 red pepper roasted (recipe follows)
- ✓ 1 yellow pepper roasted
- ✓ 1 lb Italian sausage
- ✓ 4 Portabella Mushrooms
- ✓ 4 ounces basil pesto
- ✓ olive oil
- ✓ garlic
- ✓ salt & pepper

Serves: 8 to 10
Wine: Chianti Classico or Zinfandel

- Cut roasted peppers into strips, sprinkle with olive oil and crushed garlic. Let marinate while the rest of the preparation is being done.
- Cut chicken into 1 inch cubes or ½ inch strips.
- Sauté chicken until done over medium high heat.
- At the same time grill the sausage.
- When the chicken is done mix the hot chicken with the pesto to coat.

- Set chicken and sausage aside in a warm spot.
- Slice the eggplant lengthwise into ¼ inch thick slices.
- Slice the onion into ¼ thick slices.
- Brush one side of the mushrooms, eggplant slices and onion slices with olive oil and sprinkle with salt and pepper.
- Grill or broil mushrooms, eggplant and onions over medium high heat with oiled side toward the heat.
- Grill or broil the eggplant for 3 to 4 minutes per side.
- Grill or broil the mushrooms and onions for 5 to 6 minutes per side or until done.

Note: Turn them over only once during the broiling or grilling and brush with olive oil, and sprinkle with salt and pepper after turning. As grills and broilers vary, keep a close eye on the vegetables and turn when you see a good color develop.

- Cut cheese into 8 to 12 wedges.
- Slice mushrooms into strips.
- On a bed of romaine lettuce arrange the grilled vegetables, cheese, sausage and chicken.
- Serve while still warm.

Note: leave out the chicken and sausage for a grilled veggie salad to accompany dinner.

## Roasting Peppers

- Can be done either over a gas flame or under a broiler or on a grill.
- Set whole peppers directly on the burners of a gas stove or directly under the elements of a broiler or directly over a high flame on a grill.
- Roast until skin turns black.
- Rotate each pepper until each side in roasted black.
- If necessary stand peppers on their stem end and bottom to blacken the end regions.
- When the skins are completely black remove the peppers and let cool for 10 to 15 minutes.
- Under running water, rub the blacken skins off of the peppers. A little blackened skin will remain and that is ok.
- Cut peppers into strips or slices, and place into a container that has a closed lid.
- Cover the pepper with olive oil, and ½ tablespoon of crushed garlic for each pepper.

For all of the dressings below simply mix the ingredients together with a wisk.

## *Blue cheese dressing*

- 2 cups of blue cheese crumbled by hand
- 2 cups sour cream
- 2 cups mayonnaise
- 1 tablespoon celery salt
- 1 teaspoon of chopped garlic
- pepper to taste and a little salt
- dash of Tabasco or other hot sauce

## *Thousand Island Dressing*

- 1 cup mayonnaise
- 3 to 4 tablespoons cider vinegar
- 2 teaspoons sugar
- 1/4 cup catsup
- 2 tablespoons sweet pickle relish

## *Ranch Dressing*

- ¾ cup sour cream
- ¼ cup mayonnaise
- 2 tablespoons white wine vinegar or cider vinegar
- 2 tablespoons French Vinaigrette Herbs or Herbs de Provence or other herb blend
- 1 teaspoon chopped garlic
- ½ teaspoon onion powder

- ½ teaspoon white pepper
- a little salt

## Café on the Common Vinaigrette

- 1/3 cup Rice Wine Vinegar
- 1 cup Extra Virgin Olive Oil
- Juice from 1 lime
- 2 tablespoons French Vinaigrette Herbs or Herbs de Provence or other herb blend

## Blue Cheese Vinaigrette

- ✓ 1 tablespoon Rice Vinegar
- ✓ 2 tablespoons freshly squeezed lemon juice
- ✓ 1 1/2 teaspoons minced garlic
- ✓ 2 egg yolks
- ✓ 1 tablespoon Dijon mustard
- ✓ Dash Worcestershire sauce
- ✓ 6 anchovy fillets or 1 tablespoon of Anchovy paste
- ✓ Pinch freshly ground pepper
- ✓ 1 cup pure olive oil
- ✓ About 1/4 cup crumbled Blue Cheese, Gorgonzola, Stilton or other blue cheese, plus extra for garnish
- ✓ 6 tablespoons freshly grated Parmesan, plus extra for garnish

- Put the vinegar, lemon juice, garlic, egg yolk, mustard, Worcestershire sauce, anchovies, and pepper in a blender and blend until well mixed.

- With the machine running, add the olive oil, at first by drops and then, as the mixture emulsifies, in a thin, steady stream until all the oil is incorporated.
- Pulse in 3/4 of the Gorgonzola and the Parmesan. Scrape into a bowl. Fold in the remaining Gorgonzola. Cover, and refrigerate until needed. You should have about 1 1/3 cups. (The dressing keeps, refrigerated, for 2 to 3 days.)

## *Lemon Basil Vinaigrette*

- ✓ 3 cups fresh lemon juice
- ✓ 1 shallot, coarsely chopped
- ✓ 2 cloves garlic, chopped
- ✓ 1 tablespoon honey
- ✓ 1 cup olive oil
- ✓ Salt and freshly ground pepper
- ✓ 4 basil leaves, chiffonade

  - Place lemon juice, shallot, garlic and honey in a medium saucepan and reduce to 1/2 cup.
  - Place reduced syrup into a blender, add olive oil and blend until smooth.
  - Pour into a bowl and fold in the basil.

### *Green Peppercorn Vinaigrette*
- ✓ 2 tablespoons balsamic vinegar
- ✓ 6 to 8 tablespoons extra virgin olive oil
- ✓ 1 tablespoon green peppercorns in brine
- ✓ 2 tablespoons finely minced shallots
- ✓ Salt

  - Place all ingredients in bowl or shaker and mix well

### *Dijon Vinaigrette*
- ✓ 1 tablespoon Dijon mustard
- ✓ 1 ounce red wine vinegar
- ✓ 1 teaspoon minced shallots
- ✓ 2 ounces extra virgin olive oil
- ✓ Salt and pepper, to taste

  - Place all ingredients in bowl or shaker and mix well

### *Mango Chutney*
- ✓ 2 mangoes, peeled, seeded and chopped
- ✓ 1 tablespoon fresh ginger, chopped
- ✓ 1/4 Spanish onion, chopped
- ✓ 1 tablespoon rice wine vinegar
- ✓ 2 tablespoons sugar
- ✓ 1 tablespoon cornstarch, mixed with 2 tablespoons water

  - Combine all ingredients in a saucepan.
  - Cook on low for 30 minutes.
  - Add cornstarch if desired to thicken.

## Spinach Salad with Warm Bacon Dressing

- ✓ 8 ounces young spinach
- ✓ 2 large eggs
- ✓ 8 pieces thick-sliced bacon, chopped
- ✓ 3 tablespoons red wine vinegar
- ✓ 1 teaspoon sugar
- ✓ 1/2 teaspoon Dijon mustard
- ✓ Kosher salt and freshly ground black pepper
- ✓ 4 large white mushrooms, sliced
- ✓ 3 ounces red onion (1 small), very thinly sliced

Serves 2
Wine: Pinot Grigio or Sauvignon Blanc

- Remove the stems from the spinach and wash, drain and pat dry thoroughly.
- Place into a large mixing bowl and set aside.
- Place the eggs into a covered sauce pan and cover with cold water by at least 1/2-inch.
- Turn stove on high, once the water comes to a boil, turn off heat but leave the pan covered and let the eggs sit in the water for 15 minutes.
- Immerse eggs into cold water to cool.
- Remove and peel off the shell.
- Slice each egg into 8 pieces and set aside.

- While the eggs are cooking, fry the bacon and remove to a paper towel to drain, reserving 3 tablespoons of the rendered fat.
- Crumble the bacon and set aside.
- Transfer the fat to a small saucepan set over low heat and whisk in the red wine vinegar, sugar and Dijon mustard. Season with a small pinch each of kosher salt and black pepper.
- Add the mushrooms and the sliced onion to the spinach and toss.
- Add the dressing and bacon and toss to combine.
- Divide the spinach between 4 plates or bowls and evenly divide the egg among them. Season with pepper, as desired.

Serve immediately.

## Spinach Salad with Raspberry Dressing

- 1/4 cup olive oil
- 2 teaspoons Dijon or honey mustard
- 2 teaspoons raspberry-flavored vinegar
- Freshly ground black pepper, to taste
- 1 teaspoon garlic salt
- 1 teaspoon dried basil
- 2 teaspoons sugar
- 1/8 teaspoon salt
- 4 cups baby spinach, washed well
- 4 mushrooms, sliced
- 4 strawberries, sliced
- 1/2 medium red onion, halved and sliced

✓ Candied Almonds, recipe follows
Serves 2
Wine: Pinot Grigio or Sauvignon Blanc

- In a large bowl, whisk together olive oil, mustard, vinegar, pepper, garlic salt, dried basil, sugar, and salt until dressing is well combined.
- In another large bowl, combine the spinach, mushrooms, strawberries, and red onion.
- Add the dressing and toss well.
- Sprinkle with the Candied Almonds.

## Candied Slivered Almonds:

✓ 1/2 cup sugar
✓ 1 cup slivered almonds

- In a sauté pan over medium heat, add the sugar and heat until it melts, about 6 minutes.
- Add the slivered almonds and cook until the sugar has caramelized, stirring constantly.
- Remove from the pan to a parchment lined sheet pan and cool.
- Once it has cooled, break into small pieces and set aside.

### Maple Candied Walnuts

- ✓ 1 cup split walnuts
- ✓ 1 teaspoon Cajun seasoning
- ✓ ¼ cup maple syrup
- ✓ ½ teaspoon of kosher salt
- ✓

  - In a dry non-stick pan set over medium low heat, add all ingredients.
  - Stirring frequently, cook until all liquid has evaporated and maple starts to caramelize.
  - Remove from heat and spread out on parchment paper to cool and dry, making sure pieces do not touch each other.

### Spinach Salad with Oranges and Warm Goat Cheese

- ✓ 3 small Navel oranges
- ✓ 6 ounces log of fresh mild goat cheese sliced 1/3 inch slices
- ✓ 1/3 cup walnuts finely chopped
- ✓ 1 teaspoon Dijon mustard
- ✓ 1 teaspoon rice wine vinegar
- ✓ 1/2 teaspoon kosher salt
- ✓ Pinch sugar
- ✓ 2 tablespoons extra virgin olive oil
- ✓ 1 pound spinach, trimmed
- ✓ 1 small red onion, sliced into thin rings

Serves 4
Wine: Chardonnay

- Preheat oven to 350°F.
- Cut peel and white pith from oranges with a sharp small knife.
- Working over a sieve set over a bowl, cut orange sections free from membranes, letting sections drop into sieve.
- Dip cheese slices into walnuts to coat.
- Bake on a small baking sheet in middle of oven until heated through, about 5 minutes.
- Measure out 1 tablespoon orange juice from bowl and whisk together with mustard, vinegar, salt, and sugar in a large bowl.
- Add oil and whisk until blended.
- Add spinach, onion, and orange sections to dressing and toss well.
- Season with pepper.
- Divide among 4 salad plates and carefully transfer 1 goat-cheese disk to each salad.

## *White Mountain Salad with Creole Mayonnaise Dressing*

**Dressing:**
- ✓ 1 large egg
- ✓ 2 tablespoons lemon juice
- ✓ 1/2 medium sweet Vidalia onion, diced
- ✓ 2 1/4 cups canola, vegetable, or corn oil
- ✓ 1 1/2 teaspoons hot sauce of your choice

- ✓ 1 tablespoon freshly ground black pepper
- ✓ Kosher salt, to taste

  - Place the egg, lemon juice, and onion into the work bowl of a food processor and puree.
  - With the motor running, slowly add 1/2 the oil.
  - Then add the hot sauce, pepper, and salt.
  - Stop the motor, scrape the sides of the bowl with a rubber spatula, and with the motor running again, slowly add the remaining oil.
  - Taste and adjust salt.
  - Store, covered, in the refrigerator for 1 week.

**Salad:**
- ✓ 2 hearts romaine lettuce, cleaned and torn into pieces
- ✓ 1 head bibb lettuce, cleaned and torn into pieces
- ✓ 16 ounces apple smoked bacon
- ✓ 4 eggs
- ✓ 4 ounces Gruyere cheese, shaved
- ✓ 1 1/2 cups croutons
- ✓ Salt and pepper to taste.

Serves 8
Wine: Chardonnay or a light red

  - Dice bacon and bake in 250°F oven until crisp, drain grease and hold warm.

- Place eggs in a saucepan and cover with cold water. Bring to a boil. Reduce to slow simmer and cook for 10 minutes. Remove from heat and chill in ice-bath or under running cold water. Peel and dice.
- Place lettuce in bowl. Add ¾ of bacon, ¾ of eggs. ¾ of croutons and 2 cups Creole Mayonnaise. Mix well. Season to taste.
- Divide salad onto 4 plates. Garnish with remaining bacon, eggs and crouton. Add shaved Gruyere to top of salad

## Bread Croutons:
- ✓ 1/4 pound melted butter
- ✓ 1 tablespoon fresh thyme, minced
- ✓ 1 tablespoon fresh oregano, minced
- ✓ 1 tablespoon fresh rosemary, minced
- ✓ 1 tablespoon fresh basil, minced
- ✓ 2 cups day old bread (cut into 1/8" by 1'8" inch pieces

- Mix all the herbs in butter.
- Pour butter over croutons.
- Season with salt and pepper.
- Bake in 200°F oven for 2 hours.

## *Curried Corn Salad*

- ✓ 4 ears fresh corn
- ✓ 2 teaspoons Penzey's sweet yellow curry powder
- ✓ ½ red pepper diced fine
- ✓ ¼ cup fresh chopped cilantro
- ✓ 1 ½ teaspoons kosher salt
- ✓ 1 ½ teaspoons fresh ground black pepper
- ✓ 2 tablespoons of corn, sunflower or canola oil

Serves 6 as a side dish

- Cut all kernels from the four ears of corn
- In a hot skillet add the oil and all the corn
- Stir fry on high for 5 minutes
- Add salt, pepper and curry powder
- Cook for 2 minutes more on medium low heat
- Remove from heat and cool to room temperature in a covered bowl
- Just before serving, add cilantro and red pepper, and stir to blend

Serve at room temperature or cold.

# Soups, Stews and Chili

## *Grampy Ron's Chili*
- ✓ 1 lb ground beef
- ✓ 1 large sweet onion (2" to 3" size) chopped
- ✓ 2 cloves of garlic chopped
- ✓ 2 tablespoons of olive oil
- ✓ 3 tablespoons chili powder
- ✓ ½ cup water
- ✓ 2 tablespoons ground cumin
- ✓ 1 small can of tomato paste
- ✓ 1 can of kidney beans or 1 lb dry beans cooked until tender.
- ✓ salt, pepper and cayenne pepper to taste

Serves 4-6 people
Wine: a cold beer

- In a hot dutch oven or deep pot add olive oil and chopped onion.
- Cook onion until tender.
- Add beef and brown.
- Pour off excess oil but leave some to add depth of flavor.
- Add garlic, cumin and chili powder and stir into the beef onion mixture.
- Cook spices and beef over medium heat while stirring for about 2 minutes to release spice flavors.
- Add water and cover.

- Simmer for 5-10 minutes until water is about gone.
- Add kidney beans. If using canned beans add the liquid from the can. If you are using beans you cooked from dry then add enough water to make the mixture as thick as a good stew.
- Add tomato paste.
- If the mixture is too thick add water or red wine as needed.
- Cook at a simmer for 30 minutes.

This chili improves by letting it set overnight in the refrigerator and then reheating it.

## *BearBait Chili for Jerry*

- ✓ 1 large onion, chopped
- ✓ 1 pound extra-lean ground beef
- ✓ 1 clove garlic, minced
- ✓ 1 tablespoon chili powder
- ✓ 1 teaspoon ground allspice
- ✓ 1 teaspoon ground cinnamon
- ✓ 1 teaspoon ground cumin
- ✓ 1/2 teaspoon red (cayenne) pepper
- ✓ 1/2 teaspoon salt
- ✓ 1 1/2 tablespoons unsweetened cocoa or 1/2 ounces grated unsweetened chocolate
- ✓ 1 (15-ounce) can tomato sauce
- ✓ 1 tablespoon Worcestershire sauce
- ✓ 1 tablespoon cider vinegar
- ✓ 1/2 cup water
- ✓ 1 pound spaghetti

Serves 4
Wine: Zinfandel or a cold beer

- In a large frying pan over medium-high heat, sauté onion, ground beef, garlic, and chili powder until ground beef is slightly cooked.
- Add allspice, cinnamon, cumin, cayenne pepper, salt, unsweetened cocoa or chocolate, tomato sauce, Worcestershire sauce, cider vinegar, and water.
- Reduce heat to low and simmer, uncovered, 1 hour 30 minutes.
- Remove from heat.
- Cook spaghetti according to package directions and transfer onto individual serving plates.
- Ladle Cincinnati Chili mixture over the cooked spaghetti and serve with toppings of your choice.

## *Beef Stew*

- ✓ 2 tablespoons olive oil
- ✓ 2 pounds stew beef
- ✓ 4 small yellow or white onions
- ✓ 6 red potatoes
- ✓ 4 large carrots
- ✓ 1 can tomato paste
- ✓ 1 tablespoon dry oregano
- ✓ 2 cups dry red wine
- ✓ 3 cloves garlic minced
- ✓ 2 cups beef broth

- ✓ salt & pepper

Serves 4
Wine: A hearty Cabernet Sauvignon or old vine Zinfandel

- In a large oven proof pot, brown the beef in the olive oil or medium high heat until the beef is browned on all sides.
- Add the beef broth, red wine, salt and pepper and simmer on the stove top or in the oven at 300°F for 2 ½ hours or until beef is fork tender.
- Cut onions, potatoes and carrots into pieces approximately 1 inch cubes, and add all to the pot.
- Simmer for 20 minutes.
- Add oregano, garlic and tomato paste and simmer until vegetables are tender.

Variations:
o Add parsnips in place of, or in addition to the carrots

## *Smoked Turkey and Bean Soup*

- ✓ ¼ head of cabbage
- ✓ 1 large onion
- ✓ 1 14.5 ounces can of pinto beans drained
- ✓ ¼ cup minced fresh parsley
- ✓ 1 tablespoon of hot oil
- ✓ ¼ lb smoked turkey
- ✓ 3 cups of chicken broth

- ✓ 2 tablespoon olive oil
- ✓ salt & pepper to taste

makes 4 bowls
Wine: any red will do

- Chop turkey, cabbage and onion into pieces about a ¼ inch square.
- In a hot sauce pan add the two oils.
- Add cabbage and onion to the sauce pan and cook on medium high until onion is translucent. Some cabbage and onion will brown a little in the process and this is what you want to happen.
- Add turkey and stir for 2 to 3 minutes until turkey is warmed through and you can smell the smokiness.
- Add chicken broth. Bring to a slow boil and cook for 10 minutes.
- Add drained beans and continue cooking for 5 minutes.
- Add parsley and remove from heat.

Variations:
- o Substitute smoked ham or sausage for turkey.
- o Use black or kidney beans in place of the pintos.

## *Roasted Sweet Potato and Cabbage Soup*

- ✓ 2 Sweet potatoes
- ✓ ¼ head of cabbage
- ✓ 1 tablespoon of hot oil

- ✓ 1 large onion
- ✓ 3 tablespoons olive oil
- ✓ 1 carrot
- ✓ 4 cups of chicken broth
- ✓ Salt & Pepper to taste.
- ✓ 2 tablespoons minced fresh parsley, tarragon or chives.

makes 4 bowls
Wine: white wine of your liking

- Cut each sweet potato in half lengthwise. Brush each half with the hot oil.
- In a 400° oven roast the sweet potatoes until tender, about 30 minutes.
- While potatoes are roasting, chop cabbage, onion and carrot into small pieces.
- In a hot sauce pan over medium high heat add the olive oil, and add the onion, cabbage and carrot.
- Stir fry until onion is translucent, about 10 minutes.
- Salt and pepper the vegetables while they are sautéing.
- Add the chicken broth and simmer for 10 minutes.
- When potatoes are done, remove them from the oven and scoop out the potato meat and discard the skins.
- Add the potato to the sauce pan and cook for 3 minutes.

- With an immersion blender blend the soup until smooth.
- Add salt and pepper to taste.
- Add the parsley, chives or tarragon and serve

Variations:
- You can add a dollop of sour cream at serving time.
- Add ¼ cup of heavy cream at the very end and stir in before serving.

## *Roast Squash and Sweet Potato Soup*

- ✓ 1 Acorn or similar squash
- ✓ 3 cloves garlic sliced
- ✓ 4 cups chicken broth
- ✓ 1 onion diced
- ✓ 1 sweet potato
- ✓ 2 tablespoons tarragon
- ✓ 1 tablespoon olive oil
- ✓ Salt and Pepper to taste

Serves 4 to 6
Wine: Chardonnay

- Cut the squash in half and remove seeds.
- Cut sweet potato in half, do not peel.
- Brush each with olive oil and sprinkle with salt and pepper.

- In a 375°F oven roast the squash and sweet potato until tender, about 35 to 40 minutes.
- Heat a heavy soup pot and add the olive oil and diced onion. Cook over medium heat until onion is soft.
- Scrape flesh from roasted squash and sweet potato and add to the soup pot.
- Add chicken broth and garlic
- Bring to a slow boil.
- Add tarragon
- With an immersion blender or in a blender, blend soup until desired consistency.
- Serve garnished with chopped chives or parsley

For a richer soup add ½ cup of heavy cream.

## *Roast Squash and Parsnip Soup*
- ✓ 1 Acorn or similar squash
- ✓ 3 cloves garlic sliced
- ✓ 4 cups chicken broth
- ✓ 1 onion diced
- ✓ 3 parsnips peeled and diced
- ✓ ½ cup chopped sundried tomatoes
- ✓ 1 tablespoon olive oil
- ✓ Salt and Pepper to taste

Serves 4 to 6
Wine: Vouvray or Gewürztraminer

- Cut the squash in half and remove seeds, do not peel.
- Brush with olive oil and sprinkle with salt and pepper.
- In a 375°F oven roast the squash until tender, about 35 to 40 minutes.
- Heat a heavy soup pot and add the olive oil, diced parsnips, sundried tomatoes and diced onion. Cook over medium heat until onion and parsnips are soft.
- Scrape flesh from roasted squash and add to the soup pot.
- Add chicken broth and garlic
- Bring to a slow boil.
- With an immersion blender or in a blender, blend soup until desired consistency.
- Serve garnished with chopped chives or parsley

For a richer soup add ½ cup of heavy cream.

## *Roast Squash & Yellow Tomato Soup*

- ✓ 1 Acorn or similar squash
- ✓ 3 cloves garlic crushed
- ✓ 4 cups chicken broth
- ✓ 1 onion
- ✓ 2 tablespoons tarragon
- ✓ 4 yellow tomatoes
- ✓ 2 tablespoons extra virgin olive oil

Salt and Pepper to taste

Serves 4 to 6
Wine: Pinot Grigio

- Cut the squash in half, remove seeds but do not peel.
- Cut the tomatoes in half, but do not peel.
- Brush squash and tomatoes with olive oil and sprinkle with salt and pepper.
- In a 375°F oven roast the squash and tomatoes until tender, about 35 to 40 minutes for the squash and 20 minutes for the tomatoes.
- Heat a heavy soup pot and add the olive oil, and diced onion. Cook over medium heat until onions are soft.
- Scrape flesh from roasted squash and add to the soup pot.
- Add roasted tomatoes to pot.
- Add chicken broth and garlic
- Bring to a slow boil.
- With an immersion blender or in a blender, blend soup until desired consistency.
- Serve garnished with chopped chives or parsley

For a richer soup add ½ cup of heavy cream.

## *Avocado Gazpacho*

- 3 ripe Haas avocados
- 1 cup diced seeded cucumber
- 1 cup diced seeded zucchini squash
- ¾ diced tomatoes
- ½ cup diced sweet onion
- 16 ounces chicken broth
- juice of one lemon
- 1 ½ teaspoons salt
- 1 teaspoon black pepper
- 2 tablespoons extra virgin olive oil
- 1 tablespoon Tabasco sauce or hot green salsa

Serves 4 to 6

- Place all ingredients in a food processor and process to desired degree of smoothness.

## *Lentil Soup with Ham and Potatoes*

- 2 tablespoons extra-virgin olive oil
- 3 shallots, minced
- 1 medium carrot, peeled and finely chopped
- 1 medium celery rib, finely chopped
- 1/2 cup lentils, rinsed and picked over
- 6 cups chicken stock, homemade, or store-bought reduced-sodium
- 1/2 pound red potatoes, cut into 1/2-inch dice
- 1 1/2 cups cubed ham
- Parsley puree, recipe follows

Serves 6
Wine: Merlot

- In a soup pot, heat olive oil over medium-high heat.
- Add shallots, carrot, and celery and cook, stirring occasionally, until vegetables are softened, about 5 minutes.
- Stir in lentils and chicken stock and bring to a boil.
- Reduce heat to low, cover, and simmer 10 minutes.
- Puree with immersion blender to thicken.
- Stir in potatoes and ham, cover, and simmer until potatoes are softened, 10 minutes longer.
- To serve, ladle soup into bowls and swirl in parsley puree.

**Parsley puree:**
- ✓ 3 garlic cloves
- ✓ 1/4 teaspoon salt
- ✓ 1/2 teaspoon pepper
- ✓ 1/3 cup minced fresh parsley

- Combine garlic, salt, pepper, and parsley in a blender or food processor (preferably small model) and process until pureed.

## Kale Soup

- ✓ 1 large onion, minced
- ✓ 1 large clove of garlic, minced
- ✓ 4 tablespoons olive oil
- ✓ 6 medium red potatoes, diced
- ✓ 2 qts cold water
- ✓ 6 oz of chorizo, chourico or other garlicky sausage, diced
- ✓ 2 ½ teaspoons kosher salt
- ✓ ¼ teaspoon ground black pepper
- ✓ 1 lb kale, stems removed, coursed chopped

Serves 8

- In a large heavy pot Sauté onion and garlic in 4 tablespoons of olive oil for 2 minutes or until translucent
- Add potatoes and sauté, stirring constantly for 2 to 3 minutes
- Add the water and simmer for 20 minutes or until potatoes are done
- Add sausage, salt and pepper and simmer another 5 minutes
- Add the kale and cook until tender
- Mix in last tablespoons of olive oil

## *Roasted Beet Soup*

- ✓ 2 roasted beets potatoes (see below)
- ✓ ¼ head of cabbage
- ✓ 1 large onion
- ✓ 3 tablespoons olive oil
- ✓ 4 cups of chicken broth

- ✓ Salt & Pepper to taste.
- ✓ ½ cup heavy cream

makes 4 bowls
Wine: red wine of your liking

- Cut each unpeeled beet in half and coat each half with olive oil
- Roast at 350°F until tender
- Let cool and peel
- While beets are roasting. Chop cabbage, and onion into small pieces.
- In a hot sauce pan over medium high heat add the olive oil, and add the onion, and cabbage.
- Stir fry until onion is translucent, about 10 minutes.
- Salt and pepper the vegetables while they are sautéing.
- Add the chicken broth and simmer for 10 minutes.
- When beets are done, and peeled add them.
- cook until onion and cabbage are tender.
- With an immersion blender blend the soup until smooth.
- Add heavy cream
- Add salt and pepper to taste.

## *Carrot Top Soup*

- ✓ 1 cup chopped onion
- ✓ 4 tablespoons butter
- ✓ The chopped carrot tops from 8 carrots (about 2 cups), stems removed
- ✓ 2 carrots diced
- ✓ 3 cups chicken broth
- ✓ 1/2 teaspoon minced fresh ginger
- ✓ 1 cup heavy cream or half-and-half
- ✓ 1 teaspoon caraway seeds
- ✓ 1/2 teaspoon salt
- ✓ 1/8 teaspoon pepper
- ✓ ½ teaspoon sweet curry powder
- ✓ 1 clove of garlic minced

Serves 6
Wine: Chardonnay

- In a Dutch oven, sauté onion and carrots in butter until tender.
- Add carrot tops, broth, garlic, curry powder and ginger.
- Cover and cook over medium heat for 30 minutes or until vegetables are tender.
- Cool for 15 minutes.
- Transfer to a blender, food processor or use a submersion blender, and process until smooth.
- Return all to the pan; stir in the cream, caraway, salt and pepper.
- Cook over low heat until heated through.

Serves 4 to 6
Wine: a buttery Chardonnay

- Dice the onion into 1/4 to 1/2 inch dices
- In a large pot brown the onions and mushrooms in the butter over medium high heat until onions begin to turn brown. About 10 to 15 minutes.
- Cut cod into 1 inch cubes.
- Cut scallops in half.
- Peel and cut shrimp into 3/4 inch long pieces (basically cut each shrimp into 3 equal size pieces).
- Add the olive oil to the pot.
- Add the cut up fish to the pot and stir lightly into the onions and mushrooms.
- Cook for 5 minutes stirring every now and then.
- Add clam juice and bring to a boil.
- Add heavy cream and tarragon, and bring to a boil.

Serve.

## *Trout Almandine*

- ✓ 2 Brook or Rainbow Trout, as fresh as possible, preferably never frozen, cleaned
- ✓ 1 cup sliced almonds
- ✓ 1 sliced Vidalia onion
- ✓ ¼ olive oil
- ✓ 4 sprigs of fresh dill or fenncl
- ✓ 1 lemon sliced thin into 8 slices

Serves 2
Wine: a buttery Chardonnay or Vouvray

- Preheat oven to 400°F
- Soften sliced onions over medium low heat in a little olive oil for 3 to 4 minutes.
- Remove the onions from the pan and let cool until you can handle them with your fingers
- In the same pan adds the olive oil and almonds and cook over medium low heat for 3 minutes
- Using half of the onions and almonds, stuff each trout cavity with a layer of onions, a layer of almonds, 2 slices of lemon and 2 of the sprigs of dill or fennel
- Place Trout side by side with 1 inch of space between them in an oven safe roasting pan
- Push trout cavity closed so that only one side is facing up.
- Brush with a little olive oil
- Bake in oven for 5 minutes then flip over
- Cover the trout with all remaining onions and almonds and top with 2 slices of lemon each.
- Bake for another 7 minutes.

## *Beer Battered Shrimp*

- ✓ Add 1 1/2 teaspoons cayenne pepper to beer batter (recipe below)
- ✓ 1 teaspoon salt
- ✓ A deep pot with 3 inches of peanut oil
- ✓ 1 1/4 pounds rock shrimp or peeled white shrimp

Serves 4
Wine: Vouvray

- Bring pot of oil to 350°F
- Dip each shrimp into the beer batter to coat and immediately place in hot oil
- Fry for 3 to 4 minutes, or until golden brown
- Deep fry shrimp in batches small enough so they do not bump into each other
- Continue until all are done

## *Beer Batter Coconut Shrimp*

- ✓ A deep pot with 3 inches of peanut oil
- ✓ 1 ½ pounds of shrimp
- ✓ 2 ½ cups of sweeten shredded coconut

Serves 6
Wine: Vouvray

- Bring pot of oil to 350°F
- Dip each shrimp into the beer batter (recipe below) to coat

- Roll each shrimp in the coconut and immediately place in hot oil
- Fry for 3 to 4 minutes, or until golden brown
- Deep fry shrimp in batches small enough so they do not bump into each other
- Continue until all are done

## *Beer Batter Onion Rings*

- ✓ 2 Vidalia onions, peeled and cut crosswise 1/3-inch thick and separated into rings
- ✓ Vegetable oil for deep frying
- ✓ Flour for dusting

Serves 4

- ✓ Dust the onion rings with the flour, shaking off the excess, and coat them with the beer batter (recipe below)
- ✓ Working in batches, fry the onion rings in 2 inches of preheated 370°F, oil until they are golden.
- ✓ Transfer them with a slotted spoon to paper towels to drain and sprinkle them with salt to taste.

## **Beer Batter:**

- ✓ 4 cups all-purpose flour, seasoned with salt, and pepper
- ✓ 1/2 teaspoon baking powder
- ✓ 1 egg
- ✓ 16 ounces light beer

- Mix all ingredients and set aside at least 1/2 hour.

## Tempura Batter
- ✓ 1 cup all purpose flour
- ✓ 2 teaspoons of active dry yeast
- ✓ 1 ½ cups warm water

- Mix flour and yeast in medium size bowl
- Add the warm, not hot, water and mix until just blended. Do not blend into a smooth paste, only until just blended and some lumps remain.
- Set in warm place for 60 minutes.
- Once ready it can keep in the refrigerator for up to 2 hours.

## Notes on Shrimp
**Fresh or Frozen?**
Because nearly all shrimp are frozen at sea, you have no way of knowing when those "fresh" shrimp in the fish case were thawed (unless you are on very personal terms with your fishmonger). The flavor and texture of thawed shrimp deteriorate after a few days, so you're better off buying frozen.

**Peeled or Unpeeled?**
If you think you can dodge some work by buying frozen shrimp that have been peeled, think again. Someone had to thaw those shrimp in order to remove their peel, and they can get pretty banged up when they are refrozen.

**Check the "Ingredients"**
Finally, check the ingredient list. Frozen shrimp are often treated or enhanced with additives such as sodium bisulfate, STP (sodium tripolyphosphate), or salt to prevent darkening (which occurs as the shrimp ages) or to counter "drip loss," the industry term referring to the amount of water in the shrimp that is lost as it thaws. Treated shrimp have a strange translucency and an unpleasant texture and suggest that you avoid them. Look for the bags of frozen shrimp that list "shrimp" as the only ingredient.

It's safe to say that any shrimp you buy have been frozen (and usually thawed by the retailer), but not all shrimp are the same—far from it. The Gulf of Mexico supplies about 200 million pounds of shrimp annually to the United States, but three times that amount is imported, mostly from Asia and Central and South America.

Mexican whites (Panaeus vannamei), from the Pacific coast, are usually the best. A close second, and often just as good, are Gulf whites (P. setiferus). Either of these may be wild or farm-raised. Unfortunately, these are rarely the shrimp you're offered in supermarkets. The shrimp most commonly found in supermarkets is Black Tiger, a farmed shrimp from Asia. Its quality is inconsistent, but it can be quite flavorful and firm. And even if you go to a fishmonger and ask for white shrimp, you may get a farm-raised, less expensive, and decidedly inferior shrimp from China (P. chinensis). (There are more than 300 species of shrimp in the world and not nearly as many common names.)

All you can do is try to buy the best shrimp available, and buy it right. Beyond choosing the best species you can find, there are a number of factors to consider.

Because almost all shrimp are frozen after the catch, and thawed shrimp start losing their flavor in just a couple of days, buying thawed shrimp gives you neither the flavor of fresh nor the flexibility of frozen. It is recommended that you buy frozen shrimp rather than thawed. Shrimp stored in the freezer retain peak quality for several weeks, deteriorating very slowly after that until about the three-month point. If you do buy thawed shrimp, they should smell of saltwater and little else, and they should be firm and fully fill their shells.

Avoid pre-peeled and deveined shrimp; cleaning before freezing unquestionably deprives shrimp of some of their flavor and texture; precleaned shrimp are nearly tasteless. In addition, precleaned shrimp may have added tripolyphosphate, a chemical that aids in water retention and can give shrimp an off flavor.

Shrimp should have no black spots, or melanosis, on their shells, which indicate that a breakdown of the meat has begun. Be equally suspicious of shrimp with yellowing shells or those that feel gritty. Either of these conditions may indicate the overuse of sodium bisulfite, a bleaching agent sometimes used to retard melanosis.

Despite the popularity of shrimp, there are no standards for size. Small, medium, large, extra-large, jumbo, and other size classifications are subjective and relative. Small shrimp of 70 or so to the pound are frequently labeled "medium," as are those twice that size and even larger. It pays, then, to judge shrimp size by the number it takes to make a pound, as retailers do. Shrimp labeled "16/20," for example, require 16 to 20 (usually closer to 20) individual specimens to make a pound. Those labeled "U-20" require fewer than 20 to make a pound. Large shrimp (21 to 25 per pound) usually yield the best combination of flavor, ease of preparation, and value (really big shrimp usually cost more).

One more note about size: Larger shrimp generally have larger veins, which should be removed. The veins in smaller shrimp are often so negligible that it's not worth removing them. Either way, the issue of removing the vein to be one of aesthetics. It neither harms nor improves the flavor of the shrimp.

## *Garlic Shrimp*

- ✓ 1/3 cup olive oil
- ✓ 4 garlic cloves, sliced
- ✓ 1 teaspoon red pepper flakes
- ✓ 1 pound unshelled shrimp (26 to 32 shrimp per pound)
- ✓ 2 teaspoons sweet paprika
- ✓ 1/4 cup medium-dry sherry
- ✓ 1/4 cup minced fresh parsley leaves
- ✓ Fresh lemon juice, to taste
- ✓ Salt and freshly ground black pepper

Serves 4
Wine: Chardonnay

- In a large heavy skillet set over moderately high heat, heat the oil until it is hot, add the garlic and cook, stirring, until it is pale golden.
- Add the red pepper flakes and the shrimp and cook the mixture, stirring, for 1 minute, or until the shrimp are pink and just firm to the touch.
- Sprinkle the shrimp with the paprika and cook the mixture, stirring, for 30 seconds.
- Add the Sherry, boil the mixture for 30 seconds, and sprinkle with parsley.
- Season the mixture with the lemon juice and salt and pepper, to taste, and transfer it to a serving bowl.
- The shrimp may be made up to 1 day in advance and kept covered tightly and chilled.

Serve the shrimp at room temperature.

Wine Suggestions: Dry Manzanilla; Jerez Region Spanish Cava (Sparkling Wine) Montecillo Winery Rioja

## *Grilled Garlic Marinated Shrimp with Corn and Onion Relish*

- ✓ 1 pound medium shrimp, uncooked
- ✓ Roasted Garlic Oil

- ✓ 4 cloves garlic

**Relish:**
- ✓ 5 ears of corn
- ✓ 2 bunches green onions
- ✓ 1 small red onion
- ✓ 1 lime, juiced
- ✓ 4-5 sprigs of cilantro, chopped
- ✓ Roasted Garlic Oil
- ✓ Salt and Pepper

**Sauce:**
- ✓ 1 small white onion, diced
- ✓ 1 stalk of celery, diced
- ✓ 1 small carrot, diced
- ✓ 1 red bell pepper, diced
- ✓ 2 cloves garlic, smashed
- ✓ 1/2 cup bourbon or Jack Daniels
- ✓ 1/2 cup molasses 3 cups mussel stock (clam juice or vegetable broth)

Serves 6 to 10
Wine: Chardonnay or Vouvray

- Peel and de-vein shrimp.
- Cover shrimp in garlic oil and cloves.
- Refrigerate for 20-30 minutes.
- To prepare the sauce, heat a saucepan on high heat until smoking.
- Add 2 Tablespoons garlic oil and sauté vegetables until they are brown.
- Deglaze with bourbon and reduce by half.
- Add the molasses and reduce by half.

- Add the mussel stock and reduce by half.
- Season with salt and pepper.
- Strain and serve.
- To prepare relish, coat corn with oil, salt and pepper and grill.
- Cut off the kernels and place in a bowl.
- Cut the tops off the green onions, roughly chop and put into the bowl.
- Add lime juice, cilantro, garlic oil, salt and pepper.
- Fold all ingredients together with a spoon, check seasoning and serve.
- Remove shrimp from oil, season with salt and pepper, and grill on both sides until done.

Remove and serve.

## *Fried White Anchovies with an Andalusian Pepper*

- 1 pound yellow bell peppers, roasted and peeled
- 1 pound red bell peppers, roasted and peeled
- 1/2 cup small diced Spanish onions
- 2 teaspoons chopped garlic
- 2 teaspoons Sherry vinegar
- Spanish extra virgin olive oil
- Kosher salt
- Freshly ground black pepper
- 2 pounds fresh white anchovies, eviscerated

- ✓ Flour
- ✓ Olive oil for frying

Serves 6 to 8
Wine: Pinot Grigio

- Thinly slice the peppers. In a mixing bowl, combine the sliced peppers, onions, garlic and vinegar.
- Mix well.
- Drizzle in enough Spanish olive oil to moisten the salad. Season with salt and pepper.
- Cover and refrigerate for 2 hours.
- In an electric fryer or deep pot, preheat the oil to 365°F.
- Season both the anchovies and the flour with salt and pepper.
- Dredge the anchovies in the seasoned flour, coating completely.
- Fry until golden brown and crispy, about 2 to 3 minutes.
- Remove and drain on paper towels.
- Season with salt and pepper.

To serve, spoon some of the pepper salad in the center of each serving plate. Lay the anchovies around the salad. Garnish with parsley

## *Salmon with Butter-Tarragon-Mustard Sauce*

- ✓ 2 – 6 ounce salmon filets with skin
- ✓ 2 tablespoon butter
- ✓ ½ cup dry vermouth
- ✓ honey Dijon mustard
- ✓ 1 tablespoon capers
- ✓ ¼ cup medium dry sherry
- ✓ ½ cup heavy cream
- ✓ 1 teaspoon dry tarragon

Serves 2
Wine: Chardonnay

- In a hot stick free pan add just enough oil or spray to coat pan
- cook skin side down at medium-high heat for 4 minutes
- add vermouth
- add butter
- cook covered for 5 minutes at medium heat
- add capers
- add sherry
- add heavy cream
- bring to full boil over medium heat and simmer uncovered for 3 minutes
- add tarragon and serve.

Serve with Deep fried onion & fennel (recipe in Vegetable section below)

## *Boiled Lobster*

This is for Angie, who gave me the idea.

- ✓ 2 – 1 ¼ lb lobsters
- ✓ 1 bottle chardonnay wine
- ✓ 1 tablespoon oregano
- ✓ 1 tablespoon thyme
- ✓ 1 tablespoon salt
- ✓ 1 clove garlic, minced
- ✓ ¼ lb salted butter
- ✓ 1 quart water

Serves 2
Wine: Chardonnay or champagne

- In a large pot add water and chardonnay
- Add oregano, thyme and salt
- Bring to a boil
- Add lobsters and cover
- return to a boil and cook for 10 minutes
- while lobsters cook melt butter and stir in the garlic, this is for dipping
- remove lobsters from pot and save the cooking liquid for Lobster Bisque below.
- Serve hot with melted butter to which a little fresh garlic has been added.

After the meal is complete add all left over dipping butter, lobster shells and pieces, except the liver, back to the cooking liquid. This liquid can be stored for up to 2 days refrigerated.

## Lobster Bisque

- ✓ All saved cooking liquid, dipping butter, shells and lobster pieces except the liver from the Boiled Lobster recipe above
- ✓ ½ cup heavy cream
- ✓ 2 tablespoons tomato paste
- ✓ ½ cup medium dry sherry
- ✓ 1 tablespoon tarragon
- ✓ salt & pepper to taste
- ✓ chopped chives for garnish

Serves 3-4
Wine: Chardonnay

- Bring cooking liquid to boil and cook until reduced by at least half, about 45 minutes. The more you reduce this liquid the more intense the lobster flavor will be.
- After the liquid is reduced by half strain all shells and other pieces from the cooking liquid and return the strained liquid back into the pot.
- Add tarragon and tomato paste.
- Continue cooking until reduced by half again, about 30 minutes. If you want a richer bisque then continue to cook until it reaches the desired flavor.
- Add sherry and heavy cream.
- Bring just back to a boil and remove from heat.
- Serve with chopped chives sprinkled on top

## *Lobster Cakes*

- 3 loaves of a good dense bread, remove crust and cut into medium dice
- 1 lb. red onion, small dice
- 2 red peppers, small dice
- 4 ribs celery, small dice
- 4 ounces butter, melted
- 2 cups mayonnaise
- 2 lbs. lobster meat, cooked and roughly chopped
- Salt and pepper, to taste

Serves 8
Wine: Chardonnay

- Combine all ingredients in a stainless steel or glass bowl until well mixed.
- Portion into cakes, about 2 1/2 inches in diameter and ¾ inch thick
- Heat 2 ounce. olive oil in non-stick pan and sauté until golden brown and heated throughout.

## *Spicy Tuna Tartare*

Purchase only sushi-quality tuna when preparing this recipe.

- ✓ 1 tablespoon vegetable oil
- ✓ 1 tablespoon plus 1 teaspoon soy sauce
- ✓ 1 tablespoon sesame oil
- ✓ 1 1/2 teaspoons chopped jalapeno, seeds removed
- ✓ 10 ounces sushi-quality tuna, cut into 1/8 inch dice, chilled
- ✓ 1 teaspoon grated peeled fresh ginger
- ✓ 3 tablespoons chopped green onions, green part only
- ✓ 3 tablespoons pine nuts, toasted

Serves 8
Wine: Sauvignon Blanc

- Mix the tuna, green onions, pine nuts, soy sauce, sesame oil, jalapeno, and ginger together in a medium bowl.
- Mix well.
- Keep chilled and serve within 1 hour

## *Dipping Sauce*

This sauce makes a great dipping sauce for the Fried Calamari recipe given below.

- ✓ 1/3 cup Joyce Chen Orange Spice Stir Fry Sauce
- ✓ 1/3 cup Soy Sauce

- ✓ 1/3 Sherry wine, Rice Wine or Red Wine Vinegar of your choice
- ✓ 2 tablespoons Thai or Vietnamese fish sauce
- ✓ 2 teaspoon hot pepper flakes
- ✓ 1 teaspoon grated ginger
- ✓ 1 teaspoon sugar
- ✓ 1 tablespoons chopped chives or garlic chives

- Combine all ingredients and stir until sugar is dissolved.

## *Fried Calamari*

- ✓ 1 lb Calamari cut into rings about ¼ inch thick
- ✓ 1 cup flour
- ✓ ¼ cup of Cajun spice of your choice
- ✓ large deep pan with 2 inches of peanut or canola oil (make sure pan is deep enough that the oil does not come more than halfway up the inside of the pan. When in doubt use a deeper pan.)
- ✓ Salt to taste.

Serves 3 to 4 as an appetizer
Wine: any white will do

- Heat oil to 350°F.
- In a large plastic bag or storage bag combine flour and Cajun spice.
- Slice your Calamari into rings about ¼ inch thick.

- When all the Calamari is sliced then place all of it in the bag with the flour.
- Close the top of the bag and shake until all Calamari is coated.
- When oil reaches 350°F, shake excess flour from Calamari and gently place Calamari in the hot oil. Do this in batches small enough that the Calamari is not crowded together in the pan.
- Cook 3 to 4 minutes.
- Remove Calamari from oil, drain on paper towel and sprinkle with salt.
- Cook next batch and repeat until done.

### Variation – Fried Calamari 2

Dip the calamari in Buttermilk before the flour. This gives a slightly heavier, but flavorful breading.

## *Calamari Cacciatore*

- ✓ 1 lb Calamari squid cut bodies into ¼ inch rings, leave tentacles intact.
- ✓ 4 cups of your favorite tomato sauce
- ✓ 1 large red pepper sliced into thin strips
- ✓ 1 large sweet onion sliced into thin strips
- ✓ 3 cloves garlic crushed
- ✓ 2 tablespoons of capers
- ✓ 1 cup coarsely chopped parsley
- ✓ 3 tablespoons of olive oil
- ✓ ½ pound whole wheat ziti pasta
- ✓ ¼ teaspoon crushed dry red pepper
- ✓ Salt & pepper to taste

Serves 3 to 4

Wine: a light bodied red such, as Pinot Noir or Beaujolais

- The trick to this dish is to time the pasta and calamari to be finished at the same time. If you overcook calamari it becomes very tough, so time your pasta cooking time very carefully.
- In a large hot skillet add the olive oil, immediately followed by the onions and peppers.
- Sauté at high temperature until cooked.
- Add crushed dried red pepper.
- Add tomato sauce.
- Add capers.
- Meanwhile bring a large pot of very salted water to a boil and add pasta.
- Simmer tomato sauce with onions and peppers for 5 minutes.
- When the pasta is about 3 minutes from being done, add garlic and parsley to tomato sauce.
- Then add calamari to the tomato sauce and cook for 3 minutes at a low simmer. Remove from heat.
- Drain pasta and place in pasta bowls.
- Spoon Calamari over pasta and serve.

# Meat

## Cooking Meat

Meat is muscle and is made up of two major components: muscle fibers, the long thin strands visible as the "grain" of meat, and connective tissue, the membranous, translucent film that covers the bundles of muscle fiber and gives them structure and support. Muscle fiber is tender because of its high water content (up to 78 percent). Once meat is heated beyond about 120°F, the long strands of muscle fiber contract and coil, expelling moisture in much the same way that it's wrung out of a towel. This is called denaturing. In contrast, connective tissue is tough because it is composed primarily of collagen, a sturdy protein that is in everything from the animal's muscle tendons to its hooves and/or claws. When collagen is cooked at temperatures exceeding 140°F, it starts to break down to gelatin, the protein responsible for the tender meat, thick sauces, and rich mouth feel of braised dishes.

In essence, then, meat both dries out as it cooks, i.e. meat fibers lose moisture, and becomes softer, i.e. the collagen melts. That is why, depending on the cut, meat is best either when cooked rare or cooked to the point at which the collagen dissolves completely. Anything in between is dry and tough, the worst of both worlds.

This brings us to why braising and boiling are effective cooking techniques for <u>tough cuts of meat</u>. In a recent test to determine the relative advantages of roasting, braising, and boiling, three identical cuts of beef suitable for pot roasting were cooked using the three methods. One roast was cooked in a 250°F oven, one was braised, and one was simmered in enough liquid to cover it. The results were: the roasted sample never reached an internal temperature of more than 175°F, even after four hours, and the meat was tough and dry. Both the braised and boiled roasts cooked in about the same amount of time, and the results were almost identical. Cutting the roasts in half revealed little difference; both exhibited nearly full melting of the thick bands of connective tissue. As far as the taste and texture of the meat, tasters were hard pressed to find any substantial differences between the two. Both roasts yielded meat that was exceedingly tender, moist, and infused with rich gelatin.

The conclusion? Dry heat, i.e. roasting, is ineffective because the meat never gets hot enough. It does not appear that steam heat (braising) enjoys any special ability to soften meat over boiling. Braising has one advantage over simmering or boiling, however, half a pot of liquid reduces to a sauce much faster than a full pot.

### What Happens to Meat as It Rests?

A final but very important step when cooking all red meat is allowing it to rest before slicing. As the proteins in the meat heat up during cooking, they coagulate which basically means they uncoil and then reconnect, or bond with each other, in a different configuration.

When the proteins coagulate, they squeeze out part of the liquid that was trapped in their coiled structures and in the spaces between the individual molecules. The heat from the cooking source drives these freed liquids toward the center of the meat.

This process of coagulation explains why experienced chefs can tell how done a piece of meat is by pushing on it and judging the amount of resistance: the firmer the meat, the more done it is. But the coagulation process is apparently at least partly reversible, so as you allow the meat to rest and return to a lower temperature after cooking, some of the liquid is reabsorbed by the protein molecules as their capacity to hold moisture increases. As a result, if given a chance to rest, the meat will lose less juice when you cut into it, which in turn makes for much juicier meat. In the case of beef, the texture of the meat also improves, becoming a bit firmer as it rests.

## Lamb Provencal

- ✓ 1 lb Lamb (preferably shoulder or leg or shank)
- ✓ 2 – 14 ½ ounce cans of diced tomatoes
- ✓ 3 to 4 cloves of garlic
- ✓ ½ teaspoon hot pepper flakes
- ✓ 1 can of artichoke hearts
- ✓ 1 cup sweet vermouth
- ✓ 2 cups sliced leeks
- ✓ 1 cup pitted Kalamata olives
- ✓ 1 tablespoon orégano
- ✓ 1 to 2 tablespoons of basil
- ✓ olive oil
- ✓ 1 to 2 tablespoons of fresh rosemary
- ✓ 1 teaspoon crushed black pepper
- ✓ salt to taste

Serves 2 to 3 as main dish, or 3 to 5 as a side dish.

Wine: Cabernet Sauvignon, Zinfandel or Merlot

- Dice rosemary into fine pieces.
- Cut leeks by slicing in half lengthwise and then cutting 1 inch segments of each half. Cut artichoke hearts into halves. Cut pitted olives into halves.
- Cut lamb into stew size pieces. Brown the lamb in the olive oil.
- Chop garlic and add to lamb and stir.
- Add tomatoes, hot pepper, vermouth, rosemary, back pepper. Season with salt.

- Simmer 1 hr and 15 mins.
- Add leeks, artichokes, olives and simmer for another 15 to 20 mins.
- Add oregano and basil, and serve.

Variations:
- Beef can be substituted.
- Chicken can also be used but cut first simmer to 30 mins.
- A vegetarian version can be made using eggplant in place of the lamb and cutting first simmer to 20 mins.

## *Grilled Center Cut Lamb Chops*

- ✓ 2 – center cut lamb chops for each serving desired. These chops should be 1 ½ inches thick or more.
- ✓ Cumin
- ✓ salt & pepper
- ✓ olive oil or cooking spray

Serves – as many as needed
Wine: Cabernet Sauvignon, Zinfandel or Merlot

- pre-heat oven to 425°F
- rub each lamb chop with salt & pepper and a generous portion of ground cumin
- On a hot grill coated with olive oil or cooking spray, grill the lamb chops for 4 minutes per side.

- Place grill with lamb chops into oven and roast for 15 minutes for medium rare and 20 for medium well.
- Remove from oven and let rest 10 minutes.

## *Rack of Lamb with Stilton Crust*

- ✓ 1 1/4-pound trimmed single rack of lamb (7 or 8 ribs)
- ✓ ½ cup fresh breadcrumbs
- ✓ ½ cup of Stilton cheese (you can use blue cheese as well)
- ✓ 1 clove of garlic minced
- ✓ 1 teaspoon minced onion
- ✓ 1-2 dashes of hot sauce
- ✓ 3 tablespoons olive oil
- ✓ salt & pepper

Serves 2
Wine: Cabernet Sauvignon, Zinfandel or Merlot

- Pre-heat oven to 425°F
- To the bread crumbs, add Stilton, garlic, onion, hot sauce, 2 tablespoon olive oil, crushed black pepper to taste and ½ teaspoon of salt. Mix well. If needed add extra olive oil to make cread crumb mixture stick together.
- Salt and pepper both sides of the rack of lamb
- Heat an oven safe large fry pan to medium hot
- Add 1 tablespoon olive oil

- Place rack of lamb fat side down in the fry pan and brown for 5 minutes
- Turn over rack of lamb sauté 3 minutes
- During the three minutes the backside of the rack of lamb is sautéing, use your hands or a spatula and layer the breadcrumb Stilton mixture on the fat side of the rack of lamb. Coat as even as possible
- Place fry pan with rack of lamb into the oven and roast for 20 minutes.
- Remove from oven and let rest 10-15 minutes.

## *Rack of Lamb with Cardamom and Cumin*

A low fat variation is to leave off the Stilton crust completely, and instead, sprinkle the lamb with salt, pepper, ground cardamom and cumin before browning, and then roast as directed.

## Cumin and Coriander variation

Use ground coriander in place of the cardamom

## *Lamb Shanks a la' Carol*

This is my variation of Carol LaFontaine's lamb shanks which she has so graciously served us, to our great content. Carole in turn developed this recipe from a Mediterranean recipe she modified.

- 4 lamb foreshanks
- 1 teaspoon coarsely ground black pepper
- 1 tablespoon Kosher salt
- 3 tablespoon Olive Oil
- 1 large onion, slivered
- 1 cup of chicken broth
- 2 cups of dry red wine
- 4 cloves of garlic, sliced.
- 1 cinnamon stick
- ½ teaspoon ground allspice
- 1 cup diced tomatoes, drained
- ¼ cup of fresh parsley or mint
- ½ cup dried apricots
- ½ cup dates
- ½ cup cranraisins (dried cranberries)

Serves: 4
Wine: Cabernet Sauvignon, Zinfandel or Merlot

- In a large Dutch oven brown the lamb shanks in the olive oil.
- Add the slivered onion and continue browning for 3 or 4 minutes.
- Add all dried fruit and salt and pepper.
- Add wine and chicken broth.

- Add all spices and garlic.
- Add tomatoes.
- Liquid should just cover lamb. If it doesn't add more wine or chicken stock until lamb is just covered.
- Cover and simmer on stove top or in a 350° oven for 2 ½ hours.
- At this point you can cool and store in refrigerator for up to 72 hours. When you want to serve place on stove top and bring back to a simmer for 10 minutes.
- Serve with rice, couscous or mashed potatoes.

## *Beef Tenderloin*

- ✓ Beef Tenderloin should be prepared simply and served rare.
- ✓ 1 Beef Tenderloin (2 to 3 pounds, about 3 in diameter)
- ✓ 2 tablespoons of Kosher Salt
- ✓ 2 tablespoons of Fresh Ground Pepper

Serves 8
Wine: Cabernet Sauvignon or old vine Zinfandel

- Take tenderloin out at least 2 hours before cooking time and let it come to room temperature
- One hour before cooking time season the tenderloin on all surfaces with the salt and pepper

- Pre-heat oven to 425°F and place oven rack in the middle of the oven
- When oven is hot, then in an oven proof skillet over high heat, brown the tenderloin on all sides
- Place skillet with tenderloin in the middle of your oven
- Cook until an internal temperature of 125°F. If you do not have a meat thermometer then cook for 22 minutes if the tenderloin is near 2 pounds and for 25 minutes if near three pounds
- Remove from oven, cover with aluminum foil and let rest 10 to 15 minutes before slicing.
- Serve with Red Wine and Wild Mushroom Sauce (recipe below)

## Red Wine and Wild Mushroom Sauce

- ✓ 1 tablespoon unsalted butter
- ✓ Extra-virgin olive oil
- ✓ 2 shallots, minced
- ✓ 2 pounds assorted mushrooms, such as crimini, oyster, shiitake, chanterelle, or white, trimmed and sliced
- ✓ Leaves from 2 fresh thyme sprigs
- ✓ Sea salt and freshly ground black pepper
- ✓ 1/2 cup Cabernet Sauvignon
- ✓ 1/4 cup reserved beef broth (drippings from roast) or low-sodium canned broth
- ✓ 1/4 cup heavy cream
- ✓ 1 tablespoon minced fresh chives

- Place a clean skillet over medium heat.

- Add the butter and a 2-count drizzle of oil.
- When the butter starts to foam, add the shallots and saute for 2 minutes to soften.
- Add the mushrooms and thyme; season with salt and pepper.
- Stir everything together for a few minutes.
- Add the red wine, stirring to scrape up any stuck bits; then cook and stir to evaporate the alcohol.
- When the wine is almost all gone, add the reserved beef juices.
- Let the liquid cook down and then take it off the heat.
- Stir in the cream and chives, and season with salt and pepper.

## *Pork Tenderloin New Orleans*

- ✓ 1 pork tenderloin
- ✓ 1 tablespoon Cajun spice mixture of choice
- ✓ salt & pepper
- ✓ olive oil

Serves 2
Wine: Cabernet Sauvignon, Zinfandel or Merlot

- Pre-heat oven to 400°F to 425°F
- Bring a oven safe fry pan to medium high heat

- While pan in heating evenly sprinkle all sides of the pork loin with salt, pepper and Cajun spices.
- Add olive oil.
- Brown pork for 3 minutes per side.
- Place fry pan with pork into the oven and roast for 15 minutes for medium, 18 minutes for medium well or 20 minutes for well done.
- Remove from oven and let sit 10 minutes.

## Asian Variation

Use 1 teaspoon each of ground ginger, cinnamon, white pepper and soy sauce in place of Cajun spice.

## Bronk Variation

Use 2 teaspoons each of cumin, coriander in place of Cajun spice.

## Note On Cooking Pork

Proteins are long chains of linked amino acids that fold into a huge variety of three-dimensional shapes. Folded muscle protein also holds and immobilizes a considerable amount of water in an ordered fashion. When things heat up, this organized state of affairs is thrown into disarray as the proteins unfold. Thermal analysis of pork has shown that there are three approximate temperatures at which groups of pork proteins come undone: $126°F$, $144°F$, and $168°F$. As each of these temperatures is reached, more water is freed from the proteins. Meat proteins also tend to compact as they cook, squeezing out the freed-up water.

All cooks focus on the temperature reached at the middle of a piece of meat to determine doneness, but this may be too myopic. The means by which the middle gets to that temperature is at least as important. High-heat cooking methods, such as searing, guarantee that the outer layer of meat will be well browned before the inside is just done. This works fine for the recipes above, but for pork chops the story is different. By keeping the heat level low, water loss on the outside of a pork chop is minimized, and more of the juice that is bound inside the meat remains there. And so the secret to juicy pork chops is revealed: Slow cooking over low heat is best. Also, contrary to mother's warning, pork can be served medium, and is in fact, best served less than well done.

## Southern Comfort – Maple Syrup BBQ Sauce

- ✓ 1 ½ cups tomato ketchup
- ✓ ¾ cup Southern Comfort
- ✓ ½ cup maple syrup
- ✓ 1 tablespoons whole grain mustard
- ✓ ¼ cup apple cider vinegar
- ✓ 3 cloves minced garlic
- ✓ 1 small minced Vidalia or other sweet onion
- ✓ 1/8 cup packed brown sugar
- ✓ 1 tablespoons Frank's Hot sauce or other hot sauce
- ✓ 1 teaspoon Worcestershire sauce
- ✓ ½ teaspoon salt

- ¼ teaspoon cayenne pepper
- 1 tablespoons grated ginger

  • Combine all ingredients in a food processor and process until smooth.

## *Tourtiere*

This wonderful old French Canadian pork pie recipe came to me from Bill Bronk, an old departed friend from upstate New York. It was a favorite mid-winter meal at his house.

- 2 pounds lean ground pork
- 1 cup water
- 1 cup chopped celery
- 1/2 cup chopped celery leaves
- 2 large onions, chopped
- 2 cloves garlic, chopped
- 1/2 cup chopped fresh parsley
- 1 tablespoon chopped fresh savory (or 1 teaspoon dried savory)
- ¼ teaspoon each ground cinnamon and cloves
- Salt and freshly ground pepper
- Pastry for 2 double-crust, 8-inch pies (See recipe below. If you use prepared pastry I recommend the Pillsbury product.)
- 1 egg yolk beaten with 1 tablespoon milk

Serves 8 to 10
Wine: Merlot

  • In a large, heavy saucepan over medium heat, combine pork, water,

- celery and leaves, onions, garlic, parsley, savory, cinnamon, cloves, and salt and pepper to taste. Cook, stirring occasionally, for 30 minutes, adding more water, if necessary, to prevent mixture from drying. Adjust seasoning, if necessary. Let cool.
- Line two 8-inch pie plates with pastry and fill with meat mixture. Roll out top crusts, cutting a generous vent in the centre of each. Cover each pie with top crust, trim pastry, crimp the edges to seal, and cut small steam vents. Brush top of pastry with egg yolk and milk mixture.
- Bake pies in a preheated 400°F oven for 35 to 40 minutes or until crust is golden. Serve either hot or cold.

Tip: Meat pies may be made ahead and refrigerated. Unbaked pies may be refrigerated for 24 hours, or frozen. Thaw in refrigerator before baking.

## Pastry Crust

- In a bowl, mix 2 cups sifted, all-purpose flour with 1/4 teaspoon salt.
- With pastry blender or 2 knives, cut in 3/4 cup chilled, cubed shortening or lard until mixture resembles coarse crumbs.
- Measure 1/4 to 1/3 cup ice water. Sprinkle over mixture, a spoonful at a

time, stirring with a fork, adding just enough water so dough holds together.
- Shape into a ball, press into a flat disc, wrap in plastic wrap and chill for 1 hour. Leftover pastry can be frozen for later use.

## *Veal Scaloppini and Artichoke Involtini*

- ✓ 8 cooked hearts of artichoke chopped
- ✓ 4 ounces Asiago Cheese sliced thin
- ✓ 2 tablespoons chopped parsley
- ✓ 8 veal cutlets pounded thin (about ¼ inch, called a scallop of veal)
- ✓ 4 tablespoons Olive Oil
- ✓ 5 tablespoons butter
- ✓ ¾ cup of dry white wine
- ✓ 2 tablespoons fresh squeezed lemon juice
- ✓ salt & pepper

Serves 8
Wine: Zinfandel or Merlot

- Put 2 tablespoons chopped artichokes, 2 slices of Asiago and 1 teaspoon chopped parsley onto each veal cutlet.
- Roll veal around filling and secure with a toothpick
- Season with salt & pepper
- Heat skillet to medium high heat
- Dust each veal roll (called involtini) with flour

- Into hot skillet and the olive oil and 1 tablespoon of the butter
- When butter foams add the involtini and brown on all sides (6 to 8 minutes in total)
- Transfer involtini to a dish and cover with aluminum foil
- Pour wine and lemon juice into the hot skillet and scrape all fond (the dark pieces) from the skillet bottom.
- Add 1 tablespoon chopped parsley.
- Add 4 tablespoons of butter and stir until butter is melted.
- Turn off heat.
- Season sauce with salt & pepper

To serve: remove toothpicks and pour some sauce over each involtini.

## *Osso Bucco Ragu*

- ✓ 4 (2-inch thick) veal shanks
- ✓ Salt and freshly ground black pepper
- ✓ 1/4 cup flour
- ✓ 1/4 cup olive oil
- ✓ 1 cup onion, finely diced
- ✓ 1/2 cup finely diced celery
- ✓ 1/2 cup finely diced carrot
- ✓ 1 tablespoon tomato paste
- ✓ 1/2 cup white wine
- ✓ 3 cloves garlic, peeled
- ✓ 1 (14-ounce) can crushed tomatoes
- ✓ 2 bay leaves
- ✓ 1 teaspoon dried Italian oregano
- ✓ 1 teaspoon red pepper flakes

- ✓ 1/2 teaspoon fennel seeds
- ✓ 1 bouquet garni (bundle fresh parsley stems, peppercorns and bay leaf wrapped in cheesecloth)
- ✓ 3 cups beef broth

Serves 4 to 6
Wine: Chianti Classico, Barolo or Merlot

- Season the veal shanks with salt and pepper and lightly dust each side with flour.
- Heat a large Dutch oven over medium-high heat, add the olive oil and brown the veal shanks on all sides.
- Remove the browned veal shanks to a paper towel lined plate.
- Add the onion, celery and carrots to the hot pan and cook the vegetables over a medium high heat until they are a golden brown, stirring occasionally so the vegetables do not stick to the bottom of the pan, about 6 minutes.
- As the vegetables are browning add the garlic.
- Once the vegetables have reached a golden color add the tomato paste and cook for 4 minutes.
- Deglaze the pan using the white wine, being sure to scrape all of the brown bits off the bottom using a wooden spoon.
- Add the crushed tomatoes, spices, and bouquet garni.

- Add the veal shanks back to the pan and enough beef broth to come half way up the sides of the veal.
- Cover with a lid and cook for about 3 hours, turning occasionally and adding more stock, as necessary, to keep the veal partially submerged, until the veal shanks are very tender and the meat is falling off of the bone.
- Season with salt and pepper, to taste.
- Once the veal shanks are tender, remove the shanks from the cooking liquid and, when cool enough to handle, pull the meat from the bone and shred into small pieces.
- Discard the bones and return the pulled meat to the sauce.
- Taste and re-season the sauce, if necessary.
- Serve with your favorite pasta and shaved Parmesan cheese.

## Maple Ham Glaze

For a 9 lb ham

- ✓ 1/2 cup maple syrup
- ✓ 1/2 cup dark brown sugar
- ✓ 2 tablespoons whole-grain Dijon mustard
- ✓ 1/2 teaspoon ground cinnamon
- ✓ 1/4 teaspoon ground nutmeg

- Whisk all ingredients together in a saucepan until smooth and heat over medium-low to medium heat until simmering.
- Simmer for 2 minutes and remove from heat.
- When ham is heated through, pour or brush the glaze over the top to cover completely.
- Raise oven temperature to 400°F.
- Return the ham to the oven and cook, uncovered, for 20 minutes or until glaze is caramelized and bubbly.
- Let rest for 10 minutes before slicing.

# Poultry

## *Herb Roasted Chicken*

    1 (5 to 6) pound roasting chicken
- 4 cloves garlic, crushed
- 1 medium onion, coarsely chopped
- 3 bay leaves
- 1 tablespoon each of dried thyme, rosemary and sage
- 3 tablespoons olive oil
- Salt and freshly ground black pepper to taste
- Several sprigs fresh thyme, rosemary and sage
- 1 cup chicken broth

Serves 4 to 6
    Wine: Chardonnay or Vouvray

- Preheat the oven to 425°F.
- Season the inside of the chicken cavity with salt and pepper.
- Put the crushed garlic, chopped onion and 2/3 of the dry herbs inside the cavity of the chicken.
- Use the twine and tie the legs closed.
- Rub the entire outside of the chicken with an even coat of olive oil.
- Coarsely chop remaining fresh herbs and sprinkle the herbs evenly on the chicken.

- Place the chicken into the pre-heated roasting pan and roast at 425°F for 45 minutes.
- Reduce the oven temperature to 350°F and continue to roast for an additional 1 hour.
- Remove from oven and rest on a platter for 15 to 20 minutes before carving.
- Deglaze the pan drippings with the chicken broth and de-fat as desired.
- Use a spoon to scrape up all the roasted on pieces and bring to a boil.
- Remove from the heat and strain the liquid into a gravy boat.

## *Chicken Piccata*

- ✓ 2 half chicken breasts
- ✓ ¼ cup pitted olives
- ✓ ¼ capers
- ✓ ¾ cup white wine
- ✓ 1 lemon sliced into 1/8 inch slices
- ✓ 1 clove of garlic
- ✓ unbleached flour
- ✓ ¼ cup olive oil
- ✓ salt & pepper to taste
- ✓ 1 large sauté pan, big enough to cook chicken breasts without crowding.

Serves 2
Wine: Chardonnay or a light bodied red

- Combine flour, salt & pepper and place in storage bag.

- Trim fat from chicken breasts and pound thin to about ¼ inch.
- Place chicken breasts in flour bag and shake until covered.
- Heat olive oil to almost smoking point in sauté pan and medium high.
- Shake off any excess flour and place chicken breasts in hot oil.
- Cook for 3-4 minutes per side, or until golden brown.
- Remove chicken from the pan and set aside.
- Add lemon slices to pan and brown on each side (about 1 to 2 minutes per side)
- Remove lemon from sauté pan and set aside as garnish.
- Add remaining ingredients to the pan to cook for 1 minute.
- Return chicken to pan and continue cooking until sauce has reduced by 2/3's.
- Move chicken to serving platter, pour sauce over chicken and garnish with lemon slices.

## Chicken Salad with Roasted Red Peppers

We have used different types of left over chicken in this recipe, and except for barbequed chicken any other seems to go well.

- ½ lb cold chicken meat cut into ¼ to ½ inch cubes
- 1 red pepper
- 1 clove garlic, minced
- 1 tablespoon minces sun-dried tomatoes
- 2 tablespoon mayonnaise
- dash of hot sauce of your choice
- salt & pepper

Serves 2 to 3
Wine: Chardonnay or Vouvray

- Roast the red pepper over an open gas flame until all sides are black. If you do not have a gas stove then roast the red pepper close under the broiler until blacken on all sides.
- Let roast red pepper cool to near room temperature, about ½ hour.
- Either under running water or with damp paper towels rub off the blacken skin from the red pepper.
- Discard all seeds and inner pith from the pepper.
- Cut the roasted red pepper up into the same size cubes as the chicken meat.

- ✓ 1 cup Basmati rice
- ✓ 2 cups of chicken broth

Serves 4
Wine: Merlot or Zinfandel

- Brown the carrots, onions, leeks, mushrooms and celery for 4 to 5 minutes in the olive oil.
- Stir in garlic and ginger. Sautee for 1 minute.
- Add duck.
- Add curry powder and stir in until it coats everything
- Add the coconut milk and stir in.
- Cover and bring to low simmer.
- Simmer for 15 minutes.
- Add parsley and mix in.
- While curry is simmering, bring chicken broth to a boil.
- Add rice and cook until all liquid is absorbed, stirring every couple of minutes.

To serve, place ½ cup of rice on each plate and spoon duck curry either over the rice or next to it. Serve with garlic naan.

## Roast Brined Duck

This recipe produces one of the most tender, most flavorful and least fatty ducks I've ever had.

- ✓ 1  5 to 5 1/2 pound Long Island duck
- ✓ 1 cup salt
- ✓ 1 cup sugar
- ✓ water
- ✓ ¾ cup of sweet sauce. My favorite is simply ¼ cup of Stonewall Kitchen's Peach Pomegranate Jam or the Sherry Wine Jelly from the Trappist Monks thinned with 2 tablespoons of water and heated to melt.

Serves 2
Wine: Cabernet Sauvignon

- Into a large non-reactive container add the sugar and salt and 2 pints of water.
- Mix until sugar and salt is dissolved.
- Add duck
- If needed, add enough water to cover the duck.
- Place in refrigerator for 24 hours.
- Pre-heat oven to 300°F
- Split duck lengthwise and remove the backbone
- Place duck skin side up on roasting rack in roasting pan, and place in oven.
- Roast for 3 hours
- Heat oven to 425°F

- Roast for 15 minutes or until skin is crispy.
- Coat duck skin with Peach Pomegranate Jam or Sherry Wine Jelly and return to oven 5 minutes.
- Remove from oven and let rest 5 minutes.

## Why Brining Works

Many have attributed the added juiciness of brined duck, turkey and chicken to osmosis—the flow of water across a barrier from a place with a higher water concentration, i.e. the brine, to a place with a lower one, the chicken. During roasting, poultry taken straight from the package can lose 18 percent of its original weight, while poultry soaked in water losses about 12 percent of its presoak weight. Remarkably, a brined bird will shed only a mere 7 percent of its starting weight. The benefit of brining cannot be explained by osmosis alone. Salt, too, was playing a crucial role by aiding in the retention of water.

Table salt, including Kosher salt, is made up of two ions, sodium and chloride, that are oppositely charged. Proteins, such as those in meat, are large molecules that contain a mosaic of charges, negative and positive. When proteins are placed in a solution containing salt, they readjust their shape to accommodate the opposing charges. This rearrangement of the protein molecules compromises the structural integrity of the meat, reducing its overall toughness. It also creates gaps that fill up with water. The added salt makes the water less likely to evaporate during cooking, and the result is meat that is both juicy and tender.

## *White Mountain Chicken in Wine*

- ✓ 4 slices bacon
- ✓ 2 chicken breasts
- ✓ 2 thighs
- ✓ 2 legs
- ✓ 1/2 cup flour
- ✓ Salt and pepper
- ✓ 2 cloves garlic, chopped
- ✓ 2 cups pearl onions, peeled
- ✓ 2 cups mushrooms
- ✓ 2 carrots, cut in 2-inch pieces
- ✓ 1/4 cup cognac or brandy
- ✓ 1 bottle Burgundy wine
- ✓ 2 cups chicken broth
- ✓ 5 sprigs fresh thyme
- ✓ 2 teaspoons herbs de Provence
- ✓ 3 bay leaves
- ✓ Fresh parsley, chopped, for garnish

Serves 4
Wine: Pinot Noir

- In a large, heavy skillet or Dutch oven, fry the bacon over medium heat until crisp.
- Transfer bacon to paper towels to drain.
- Coat chicken pieces in flour, salt and pepper.
- Brown chicken in hot bacon fat on both sides.

- Add garlic, onions, mushrooms and carrots. Saute 2 minutes to soften.
- Pour cognac into a small glass. Remove pan from heat, pour in cognac, put pan back on the flame. Flambe by lighting a long match and holding it just above the pot and light the fumes. The brandy will catch fire and the flames will burn out within 1 minute.
- When the flames die down, gradually stir in the wine and broth.
- When the wine is well blended, add the herbs.
- Cover and simmer for 1 hour. Remove cover and continue to simmer for 15 minutes to allow the sauce to reduce a bit.
- You may want to add 1 tablespoon of tomato paste or cornstarch to aid in the thickening process.
- To serve, top the chicken and vegetables with reserved crumbled bacon and fresh parsley.

## *Chicken with Tortellini and Sun Dried Tomato Pesto*

- ½ lb fresh cheese or mushroom tortellini (do not use dried tortellini)
- 2 tablespoon olive oil
- ½ lb fresh mushrooms, quartered, baby bellas are my preference
- 4 tablespoon sun dried pesto
- 1 minced clove of garlic
- 1 shallot minced

- ✓ 1 tablespoon capers
- ✓ ¼ cup heavy cream
- ✓ 1 cup chopped fresh parsley
- ✓ salt & pepper
- ✓ 1 lb of boneless chicken breast or thighs cut into 1 inch cubes

Serves 2
Wine: any dry red

- Brown the chicken in the olive oil until done.
- Stir in garlic and shallot and cover.
- Remove from heat and let stand.
- While the pasta cooks sauté the mushrooms in the olive oil for 5 minutes on medium high heat
- Add the capers
- Sauté for 3 minutes on medium heat
- Add cream and sun dried tomato pesto
- Bring just back to a simmer and remove from heat.
- Cook the pasta in plenty of salted boiling water until tender
- Drain pasta
- In a large bowl place pasta, parsley and pour sauce over pasta and mix.

Serve with fresh grated Parmigiano Reggiano cheese

## *Poulet a la Crème avec Jerez*

- ✓ 1 lb boneless, skinless chicken breasts
- ✓ 1/3 cup Sherry
- ✓ ½ cup tomato paste
- ✓ ¼ cup sundried tomatoes diced
- ✓ ¼ cup capers
- ✓ 1/3 cup heavy cream
- ✓ salt & pepper
- ✓ 2 tablespoons of olive oil
- ✓ ½ lb cooked pasta of choice

Serves 2
Wine: Chardonnay

- Cut chicken into strips or ½ inch cubes.
- In a large fry pan or skillet brown the chicken in the olive oil over medium high heat until browned on all sides and cooked through.
- Add the tomato paste, capers and sundried tomatoes and stir to coat chicken
- Add the sherry and allow alcohol to evaporate.
- Add the cream and stir until sauce is even consistency.

Serve over your favorite pasta, we recommend tortellini.

## Chicken Pot Pie

- ✓ 1 lb of boneless and skinless chicken thighs cut into ¾ inch cubes
- ✓ 1 lb of boneless and skinless chicken breasts cut into ¾ inch cubes
- ✓ 4 red potatoes cut into ¾ inch cubes
- ✓ 4 carrots cut into ¾ inch pieces
- ✓ 2 Stalks of celery cut into ¾ lengths
- ✓ 1 large sweet onion cut into ¾ inch pieces
- ✓ 3 cups of chicken stock
- ✓ 5 tablespoons all purpose flour
- ✓ 4 tablespoons butter
- ✓ 2 tablespoons poultry seasoning
- ✓ Salt & Pepper to taste
- ✓ Olive oil for sautéing
- ✓ A deep Dutch oven or oven safe pot
- ✓ One pastry crust (see recipe in index)

Serves 8
Wine: Chardonnay

- Over medium high heat, using the Dutch oven brown the chicken in the olive oil
- Remove the chicken and set aside, in the same pan sauté the potatoes, carrots and onions for 10 minutes.
- Add the chicken back into the pan and mix together.
- Add salt and pepper to your taste
- Add the poultry seasoning and mix it in.

- Add the chicken broth and bring to a simmer
- Simmer for 15 minutes
- While the chicken simmers, melt the butter over low heat in a separate small sauce pan
- When the butter has completely melted, stir in the flour until it is smooth.
- After the chicken has simmered for 10 minutes, stir in the butter/flour mixture and keep stirring until it has melted into the chicken stock.
- Bring back to a simmer and cook until the broth thickens.
- If there is a little too much thicken broth remove some with a large spoon until there is not quite enough to cover the chicken and vegetables
- At this point taste and adjust seasonings if needed.
- Remove from the heat, and let cool while oven preheats.
- Turn on oven and preheat to 350°F
- When the oven is at temperature, roll out the pastry crust until you have a round piece slightly larger in diameter than your Dutch oven
- Place pastry crust into the Dutch oven and down onto the chicken and vegetables (some of the pastry may be pushed up along the edges, simply fold back onto the top crust as a boarder)

- Pierce the crust with several small slits (you can give the crust a milk or egg wash at this point if you wish)
- Place in oven and bake for 30 to 40 minutes or until top is golden brown.

## *Apricot Ginger Glazed Chicken with Chipotle Sweet and Red Bliss Potatoes*

- 8 chicken thighs
- 1 jar apricot jam
- 1 teaspoon grated fresh ginger
- ½ cup honey
- ¼ cup soy sauce
- 1 Tablespoons minced garlic
- ¼ cup chopped scallion
- 3 large sweet potatoes, peeled and cubed
- 5 red bliss potatoes, cubed
- 3 chipotle chiles from the can
- Non-stick cooking spray
- 1 tablespoon Extra Virgin Olive Oil
- salt and pepper to taste

Serves 4
Wine: Chardonnay or Vouvray

- Heat oven to 350°F and par-bake chicken thighs (approx 30-40 minutes).
- Prepare glaze by whisking together apricot jam, ginger, honey, soy sauce, minced garlic, and chopped scallion.
- Spray a large baking dish with non-stick cooking spray.

- In a large bowl combine potatoes, chipotles, olive oil, salt, and pepper.
- Pour into baking dish and bake until tender, about 40 minutes.
- To finish chicken, heat grill and grill chicken on both sides, brushing with glaze till done.

# Pasta

## *Basic Tomato Sauce*

Tomato sauce should be kept simple. Otherwise, the flavors become all jumbled and unrecognizable. I have a friend who thinks that almost anything can go in a tomato sauce and I cringe every time she offers me some. The recipe below is for basic tomato sauce. Once created you can add what you like, or use as you like, to create a plethora of dishes.

- ✓ 5 lbs of fresh plum tomatoes stems cut out and quartered. For heaven sake leave the skins on that's where all the flavor, fiber and vitamins are.
- ✓ 3 cloves of garlic chopped
- ✓ 1 large sweet onion chopped
- ✓ 1/4 cup olive oil
- ✓ 2 tablespoons kosher salt
- ✓ 2 tablespoons dried Turkish oregano
- ✓ 1 teaspoon black pepper
- ✓ 2 cups red wine (optional)

Serves many

- In a large pot add the olive oil and onions and cook over medium heat until the onions are translucent.
- Add the tomatoes and salt.

- Cover the pot and let cook for 10 to 15 minutes over medium low heat. Stir every couple of minutes to make sure tomatoes do not stick to the bottom and burn.
- When the tomatoes have released their juices the pot will be filled with simmering tomatoes in plenty of liquid. Now add the red wine (optional), oregano, garlic and black pepper.
- Cook covered over medium low heat for another 30 minutes.
- Remove cover and simmer for another 30 minutes.
- Use a submersible blender and blend all the pots contents until smooth.
- Continue to cook on medium low heat uncovered until sauce thickens to the point you like. If you do not have the time to thicken the sauce by slow simmering, then add a high quality tomato paste to thicken.

Place in 1 pint containers and freeze until needed. When needed thaw and add the flavorings you want while reheating. If you use basil, add that just before serving as it will lose its flavor if you add it too soon.

## *Pasta Dough*

To make one pound of pasta, you need
- ✓ 2 cups of unbleached flour
- ✓ 3 large eggs
- ✓ 1/2 teaspoon of salt.

- Place the flour on a table in a mound and make a well in the center.
- Put the eggs and salt into the well.
- Mix the eggs together with a fork without disturbing the flour any more than necessary.
- Using a fork, gently incorporate the flour into the egg mixture a little at a time.
- Once you have incorporated all of the flour together with the egg using a fork, switch to a bench knife or use your fingertips to blend the mixture together well.
- After the wet and dry ingredients have been combined, bring the mixture together with your hands to form a ball.
- If the dough seems to dry, add a little more egg mixture.
- If the mixture is too wet and sticks to your fingers, rub your hands with flour and form the dough into a ball.
- Knead the pasta dough as you would bread dough. Pushing down and away from you with the palm of your hand. Turn the dough ninety degrees, fold the dough over on itself and push down and away again. Continue this until the dough is smooth, about 7 minutes.
  Cut the dough into 3 equal sections.
- Form each section into a ball.
- Cover the dough balls with a towel or bowl and let rest for 15 minutes.

- Pasta machines are great for rolling and cutting the dough. They are inexpensive and can be found at major kitchen stores or online. If you don't have a pasta machine, a rolling pin will work just fine.
- Flatten one of the dough balls with the palm of your hand until it's about 1/2 an inch thick and no wider than the slot of the pasta machine.
- With the slot of the pasta machine on its widest setting, usually 1; turn the handle while feeding the dough into the slot.
- Gently hold the flattened dough as it comes out of the pasta machine, but don't pull on it.
- After the dough has completely passed through the pasta machine, turn the slot down to the next smallest setting and pass the dough through the slot.
- Continue to do this, making the slot smaller by one each time.
- Don't try to skip a number, as this will only cause the machine to jam and you'll end up with a mess and no pasta.
- As you continue rolling the pasta, your sheet of dough will get longer and longer.
- Try to gently hold the dough as it exits the pasta machine so it doesn't tear.

- Continue passing the dough through the machine until it's about an 1/16th of an inch thick.

## *Lobster Ravioli*

- ✓ 1 clove garlic, chopped
- ✓ 1 tablespoon chopped shallots
- ✓ 16 ounces cooked lobster meat
- ✓ 2 ounces Cognac
- ✓ 8 ounces cream cheese
- ✓ salt & pepper
- ✓ 1 tablespoon chopped chives
- ✓ 1 pound of pasta rolled into thin sheets (see recipe above)
- ✓ A small bowl of water

Serves 6
Wine: Chardonnay

- Combine the garlic, shallots, lobster, cognac, cream cheese, chives, salt and pepper and blend in a food processor until lobster is in small pieces but nor pureed.
- Lay out flat one sheet of pasta
- Using a melon baller, place a scoop of the lobster filling in a roll down the centerline of the pasta sheet, with one scoop every four inches.
- Using your finger, make wet with the water a line completely around each scoop
- Place another sheet of pasta on top of the first sheet

- Press the top sheet around each scoop. The water you wet the bottom sheet with will seal the top and bottom sheets together.
- With either a ravioli cutter or sharp knife, cut around each scoop leaving at least ½ inch of pasta around each scoop
- Insure each ravioli is sealed by pressing the edges together with your fingers or a fork
- Save the leftover pasta pieces from cutting out all of the ravioli and form back into a ball and run through the pasta roller again to make more ravioli.

## *Grampy Ron's Mac & Cheese*

- ✓ 1 pound elbow macaroni
- ✓ 6 tablespoons butter
- ✓ 6 tablespoons flour
- ✓ 2 tablespoon powdered mustard
- ✓ 5 cups milk
- ✓ ½ cup sweet onion, finely diced
- ✓ 2 bay leaf
- ✓ 1 teaspoon paprika
- ✓ ½ teaspoon of ground nutmeg
- ✓ ½ cup chopped fresh parsley
- ✓ 2 large eggs
- ✓ 8 ounces sharp cheddar shredded
- ✓ 8 ounces Gruyere shredded
- ✓ 8 ounces of Monterey Jack shredded
- ✓ 3 teaspoon kosher salt
- ✓ Fresh black pepper
- ✓ Topping:

- ✓ 6 tablespoons butter
- ✓ 3/4 cup panko bread crumbs

Serves eight to ten
Wine: any dry wine

- Preheat oven to 350°F.
- Sauté onion until translucent and then set aside.
- Cook the pasta to al dente.
- Make the roux: In a 5 quart pot, melt the butter and immediately whisk in the flour and mustard and whisk continuously for four to five minutes over medium low heat.
- Stir in the milk, onion, bay leaf, nutmeg and paprika. Simmer for eight to ten minutes until roux thickens and then remove the bay leafs.
- Temper in the egg by stirring four 1 tablespoon portions of the roux into the eggs one at a time. Then add the eggs to the roux while stirring.
- Stir in 3/4 of the cheese.
- Season with salt and pepper.
- Add parsley.
- Fold the macaroni into the mix and pour into a 5-quart casserole dish.
- Top with remaining cheese.
- Melt the butter in a sauté pan and stir in the bread crumbs to coat.
- Top the macaroni with the bread crumbs.
- Bake for 30 minutes.

- Remove from oven and let rest for ten minutes before serving.

## *Elicoidali with mushroom sauce*

Elicoidali resembles a small ziti, but any pasta you like could be used.

- ½ Elicoidali pasta
- 2 tablespoon olive oil
- ½ fresh mushrooms, quartered, baby bellas are my preference
- 2 tablespoon julienne sun dried tomatoes that have been packed in oil
- 1 minced clove of garlic
- 1 tablespoon capers
- ¼ cup heavy cream
- ¼ cup basil pesto, use the fresh kind now being sold in stores everywhere
- salt & pepper

Serves 2
Wine: any dry red

- Cook the pasta in plenty of salted boiling water
- While the pasta cooks sauté the mushrooms in the olive oil for 5 minutes on medium high heat
- Add the sun dried tomatoes, garlic and capers
- Sauté for 3 minutes on medium heat
- Add cream and pesto
- Bring just back to a simmer and remove from heat.

- Drain pasta
- Pour sauce over pasta and mix.
- Serve with fresh grated Parmigiano Reggiano cheese

## *Tortellini variation*

Use 1 lb fresh mushroom & cheese stuffed tortellini in place of the Elicoidali.

## *Grilled Vegetable Lasagna with Puttanesca Sauce and Pesto*

- 2 pounds ricotta
- 1 teaspoon salt
- basil pesto (use homemade or prepared pesto sauce of good quality)
- 1/2 cup Extra Virgin Olive Oil
- Puttanesca Sauce, recipe follows
- 1 1/4 pounds lasagna noodles
- Grilled vegetables, recipe below in chapter on vegetables
- 8 ounces mozzarella, coarsely grated

Serves 8 to 10
Wine: Chianti Classico or Barolo

- Preheat oven to 350°F.
- In a medium bowl mix the ricotta cheese with salt, half a cup of Pesto and half a cup of olive oil
- Lightly grease a large rectangular baking dish, then spoon 1/2 cup of Puttanesca Sauce onto the bottom of

the dish. Cover with a layer of lasagna noodles. Top the lasagna with a layer of ricotta, then a layer of eggplant, zucchini, onion and red pepper, a layer of grated mozzarella, and a layer of puttanesca sauce. Repeat layering the lasagna, ricotta, vegetables, mozzarella and sauce in this manner until all ingredients have been used, ending with mozzarella on top.
- Bake until the lasagna is bubbling and golden brown, about 1 hour and 15 minutes. Allow to rest 10 minutes before serving, drizzled with some of the remaining pesto oil.

## Puttanesca Sauce:
- ✓ 1/4 cup olive oil
- ✓ 1 cup finely chopped onion
- ✓ 6 cloves minced garlic
- ✓ 2 (28-ounce) cans Roma plum tomatoes, broken into pieces, with juice
- ✓ 1 cup tightly packed, pitted, chopped Kalamata olives
- ✓ 2 tablespoons tomato paste
- ✓ 2 tablespoons drained capers
- ✓ 2 tablespoons (about 8) minced anchovy fillets
- ✓ 1/2 teaspoon dried crushed basil
- ✓ 1/2 teaspoon dried crushed red pepper flakes

Salt

- In a large pot heat the olive oil over medium high heat.
- Add the onion and saute until soft and lightly caramelized, about 6 minutes.
- Add the garlic and cook an additional 2 minutes.
- Add the tomatoes and the remaining ingredients and simmer until the sauce is thickened and slightly reduced, about 40 minutes.
- Adjust seasoning to taste, cover and set aside.

# Vegetables

## *Sweet Potato and Parsnip Hash*

- ✓ 1 large sweet potato
- ✓ 3 parsnips
- ✓ 1 medium size onion
- ✓ 1 tablespoon olive oil
- ✓ 2 tablespoon salted butter
- ✓ 1 tablespoon dry tarragon
- ✓ salt & pepper

Serves 2 to 3
Wine: Vouvray

- Chop sweet potato, parsnips and onion into ¼ cubes or julienne strips
- Add olive oil to medium hot pan
- Add onions to pan and caramelize for ten minutes
- Add butter to the pan.
- Add potato and parsnips to the pan
- Salt & pepper to taste
- Sauté over medium until potato is tender, about 12 minutes
- Remove from heat and stir in tarragon

## *Mashed Sweet Potatoes*

- ✓ 2 sweet potatoes
- ✓ 4 tablespoon butter
- ✓ 1 cup grated Parmigiano Reggiano or other hard Italian cheese
- ✓ ½ cup heavy cream
- ✓ 1 tablespoon marjoram, oregano or tarragon
- ✓ salt & pepper

Serves 4
Wine: Vouvray

- Either bake or boil the sweet potatoes in their skins until tender.
- While still hot, scoop the potatoes from their peels with a large spoon.
- In either a food processor or hand processor, add potatoes and remaining ingredients and process until mixed. Do not over process.

## *Grilled Vegetables*

- ✓ 4 medium zucchini, cut lengthwise into 1/4-inch slices
- ✓ 4 red or yellow bell peppers, roasted, seeded and peeled
- ✓ 2 medium eggplants (about 1 1/2 pounds), cut into 1/4-inch rounds
- ✓ 2 large yellow onions, cut into 1/4-inch rounds

1/4 cup extra virgin olive oil

## *Eggplant Stew*

- ✓ 1 large eggplant cut into 1 inch cubes
- ✓ 1 large onion cut into 1 inch squares
- ✓ 1 large yellow or red pepper cut into 1 inch squares
- ✓ ½ lb mushrooms quartered
- ✓ 3 cloves of garlic, chopped
- ✓ 1 tablespoon dry oregano or 2 tablespoon chopped fresh oregano leaves
- ✓ 1 teaspoon thyme
- ✓ 1 tablespoon fresh chopped rosemary leaves
- ✓ 1 tablespoon dry basil or 2 tablespoon chopped fresh basil
- ✓ 1 can of good quality whole tomatoes with juice
- ✓ 4 tablespoon olive oil
- ✓ salt & pepper

Serves 3-4
Wine: Merlot or Chianti Classico

- In large pot add olive oil and heat to medium
- Add eggplant and sauté for 5 minutes, if eggplant absorbs all the oil add 2 more tablespoon.
- Add onion, pepper and mushrooms and sauté another 10 minutes
- While vegetables are sautéing, crush whole tomatoes with your hands and save all juice.
- Add garlic and sauté 1 minute

- Add tomatoes and juice
- Add all herbs and simmer until eggplant is very tender, about 10 minutes
- Serve with crusty bread and cheese selection

## *Deep Fried Fennel and Onions*
- ✓ 1 bulb of fresh fennel (anise)
- ✓ 1 large sweet onion like a Vidalia onion
- ✓ Corn or Peanut oil as needed (see below)
- ✓ 1 tablespoon Cajun spice of choice
- ✓ 2 cups flour
- ✓ 1 tablespoon of salt
- ✓ 1 tablespoon ground pepper
- ✓ 2 cups of milk

Serves 3-4
Wine: any dry white

- Slice onion and fennel into ¼ wide strips, not rings
- Soak the onion and fennel in the milk for 20 minutes. If more milk is needed to cover the vegetables then add whatever is needed to cover.
- In your pan of choice (at least 4 inches deep) add 2 inches of corn or peanut oil
- Heat oil to 350°F
- Into a large zip lock bag add the flour, Cajun spice, salt and pepper
- After the vegetables have soaked for 20 minutes add one handful into the flour mixture, close bag and shake.

- Shake off residual flour and carefully place vegetables into the hot oil.
- The oil will foam up but the foam will subside.
- If you are using a large pan then add another breaded handful, if not cook in batches. Do not over crowd the pan.
- Stirring occasionally, fry until golden brown, about 5 minutes.
- Remove from oil and place into paper towel lined tray. Sprinkle with salt immediately.
- Repeat steps until all vegetables are cooked.

## *Red Onion Confit*

Sometimes called Red Onion Marmalade.

- ✓ 10 large red onions
- ✓ 2 cups balsamic vinegar
- ✓ 1 cup honey
- ✓ 1 tablespoon kosher salt
- ✓ 1 tablespoon black pepper

- Cup onions into strips
- In a large covered pot combine onions, balsamic vinegar, honey, salt and pepper.
- Cook covered for 30 minutes.
- Remove cover and simmer another 30 minutes until the liquid level reduces by a third and the consistency of the mixture approaches that of marmalade.

Store in airtight containers in the refrigerator and then reheat as needed. Will store for up to two weeks.

## *Patatas Catalan*

- ✓ 8 small red potatoes per serving
- ✓ 1 clove garlic, chopped
- ✓ 1 shallot, chopped
- ✓ 2 tablespoons Olive Oil
- ✓ ½ cup Chicken Broth
- ✓ ¼ cup fresh parsley, chopped

Serves 2
Wine: light bodied red or any dry white

- Cut potatoes into quarters, do not peel.
- In a heavy fry pan, brown the potatoes in the olive oil over medium heat until almost done (about 10 minutes)
- Add the garlic and shallot and continue frying until garlic is light golden but not brown.
- Add chicken stock and cover pan immediately.
- Cook for 5 minutes
- Remove cover and continue cooking until all water has evaporated.
- Add parsley and serve.

## *Onion Chutney*

- ½ cup water
- 1 large sweet onion chopped
- ¼ cup of currants
- ¼ dried cherries
- ¼ cup cranraisins
- ¼ dried apricots chopped
- 1/8 teaspoon cayenne
- ½ teaspoon salt
- ½ teaspoon sweet curry powder
- 1 teaspoon brown sugar
- ¾ cup apple juice or cider

- In a sauce pan add water, onion, currants, cherries, cranraisins, apricots, cayenne and salt.
- Cook over medium-low heat until the mixture is nearly dry.
- Add curry, brown sugar and apple juice
- Continue cooking until mixture is thick like a jam.
- Let cool and package in air tight contain and refrigerate.

Can be stored in refrigerator for up to 2 months.

# Grape Varieties and the Wines They Produce

## *White Grapes:*

- **Chardonnay**: One of the most widely planted and recognized white grapes in the world, Chardonnay can produce a wide range of styles but tends to produce medium to full-bodied whites that can be quite complex.
- **Chenin Blanc**: Best known for its role in the Loire Valley of France, Chenin is the grape of Vouvray and Savennières amongst others.
- **Gewurztraminer**: An often misunderstood wine, the flamboyant personality of Gewurz can either make you love it or hate it on first sniff.
- **Pinot Grigio**: A very popular grape for simple dry white wines.
- **Pinot Gris**: Although it is technically the same grape as Pinot Grigio, the wines made from Pinot Gris in Alsace in France are fruitier.
- **Riesling**: Riesling is capable of producing some very good wines from dry to very sweet.
- **Sauvignon Blanc**: Another widely planted and popular white grape, Sauvignon Blanc is often seen as the yin to Chardonnay's yang.

## *Red Grapes:*

- **Cabernet Franc**: Often used as a blending grape with other Bordeaux varietals, Cab Franc is also used as a principal grape in the Loire Valley of France and in a few wines of Bordeaux's Right Bank.
- **Cabernet Sauvignon**: Probably the most well known red grape in the world, Cabernet is the most important grape of the Left Bank wines of Bordeaux and is widely planted in California, Australia, Italy and others places.
- **Grenache**: Until recently, this grape was not as widely known. But with the explosion of interest in Chateauneuf-du-Pape and other Rhone wines, its popularity has spread and now there are many examples from Spain's Rioja region to California and Australia.
- **Merlot**: The second most famous wine of Bordeaux, Merlot is often used in blends with Cabernet Sauvignon or as a principal grape in wines from the Right Bank and in many other regions such as California, Italy and others.
- **Sangiovese**: One of the top two red grapes (the other being Nebbiolo) in Italy, believed to have originated in Tuscany, where it dominates today. Sangiovese wines are typically high in acid, have moderate to high tannins and a flavor that's lightly fruity with a hint of earthiness.

Most are not long-lived and will last for less than 10 years. One strain of Sangiovese is Brunello ("little dark one"), the grape responsible for the potent and long-lived brunello di montalcino. Sangiovese is the dominant grape in Italy's chianti wines.
- **Nebbiolo**: While its use in other regions around the world has been slow to catch on, Nebbiolo is still considered one of the most noble grape varieties because it is the grape that produces Barbaresco and Barolo in Piedmont Italy.
- **Pinot Noir**: Pinot Noir is a noble variety best known for being the grape of red Burgundy. It is a difficult variety capable of making some of the best wines in the world. Old world Pinots from Burgundy can be deep and rich, and very expensive. In recent times Pinot is usually a light wine. It is widely planted and examples from California, Oregon and others are very popular.
- **Syrah**: The grape of the northern Rhone Valley in France, Syrah is the main grape in the wines of Hermitage, Cote Rotie and others. It has become popular elsewhere as well, making rich, structured wines in California and Australia, where it is known as Shiraz.

# Index

Almonds, candied, 64
Anchovies, 99
Avocado
  Gazpacho, 80
Batter
  Beer, 92
  Tempura, 93
BBQ Sauce, 121
Beans
  Black Bean Hummus, 27
  Black Beans, 27
  Hummus, 27
Beef
  Asian Skewers, 26
  Chili, 70
  ground, 36, 70, 71, 72
  Ground - Meatballs, 36
  Provencal, 113
  Roast Beef Salad, 25
  Stew, 72
  Tenderloin, 117
Beef Stew, 72
Blue Cheese
  Shortbread with Walnuts and Chutney, 18
Bread
  European Style, 41, 133
  Hushpuppies, 50
  Oatmeal Orange Sweet Potato, 50
  Portuguese Cornbread, 52
  Sour Dough, 43
  White Mountain Cornbread, 47
Brining Poultry, 137
Calamari, 39, 106
Calamari, 107
Cheese
  Asiago, 124
  Blue Cheese, 14, 17, 18, 25, 59, 114
  Blue Cheese Dressing, 58
  Blue Cheese Vinaigrette, 59
  Cheddar, 151
  Feta-Mint Dip with Yogurt, 33
  Fontina, 12, 13
  Goat Cheese, 38, 39, 65
  Gorgonzola, 14, 18, 25, 60
  Gorgonzola, 59
  Gruyere, 35, 36, 67, 68, 151
  Monterey Jack, 19, 151
  Mozzarella, 154, 155
  Mozzerella, 19
  Parmigiano Reggiano, note on, 23
  Parmigiano-Reggiano, 15, 20, 21, 23, 24, 25, 46, 135, 140, 154, 158
  Provolone, 55
  Stilton, 114, 115
  Stilton, 59
Chicken

Apricot Ginger Glazed, 144
Breast, 130
Curry, 133
Grilled for Antipasti, 55
In cream sauce with Sherry, 141
in wine, 138
Piccata, 130
Pot Pie, 142
Provencal, 113
Roasted with herbs, 129
Salad with Roasted Red Peppers, 132
with Tortellini and Sun Dried Tomato Pesto, 139

Chili
BearBait Chili, 71
with beef and beans, 70

Chutney
Onion, 165

Chutney, Mango, 61

Dressings
Blue Cheese, 58
Dijon Vinaigrette, 61
Green Peppercorn Vinaigrette, 61
Lemon Basil Vinaigrette, 60
Ranch, 58
Thousand Island, 58
Vinaigrette, Café on the Common, 59

Duck
Brined and Roasted, 136
Curry, 134

Fabbri, Nancy, 10

Fish
Anchovies, 99
Anchovies, 99
Calamari, 39, 40, 105, 106, 107, 108
Calamari Fried, 105
Crab, 86, 87, 88
Lobster, 102, 103, 150
Lobster, Bisque, 103
Lobster, Cakes, 104
Salmon, 34
Scallops, 88, 89
Shrimp, 16, 17, 19, 88, 89, 91, 92, 93, 94, 95, 96, 97, 98, 99
Shrimp, Beer Battered, 91
Shrimp, Beer Battered Coconut, 91
Shrimp, Garlic, 96
Shrimp, Grilled Marinated, 97
Trout, 89
Tuna, 105

Fish Cakes
Crab Cakes with Curry Sauce, 86
Fish Cakes, 85
Lobster Cakes, 104

Fontina, 12

Garlic
Note on Garlic, 28

Gazpacho
Avocado, 80

LaFontaine, Carol, 25, 116

Lamb
Chops, 113
Provencal, 112

Rack of with Stilton, 114
Rack of, with Cardamom and Cumin, 115
Rack of, with Cumin and Coriander, 115
Shanks, 116
Lobster
  Bisque, 103
  Boiled with wine, 102
Meat
  Cooking, 109
  Resting after cooking, 110
Meatballs in Tomato Garlic Sauce, 36
Mushrooms, 15
  Baby Bella, 15
  Crimi, 15
  In Puff Pastry, 15
  Portabella, 55
  Portabella, 21
Olives
  Kalamata, 30
  Nicoise, 30
  Note on Black Olives, 29
  Tapenade, 30
Pancakes
  Blueberry, 45
  Corn Cakes, 45
  Fluffiness, 45
  Oat Cakes, 45
  Pecan, 45
  White Mountain, 44
Pasta
  Dough, 147
  Elicoidali with mushroom sauce, 153
  Lobster Ravioli, 150
  Pasta with mushroom sauce, 153
  Tortellini with mushroom sauce, 154
Pastry Crust, 123
Peppers
  Roasting, 57
Pesto
  Sundried Tomato, 21, 22
Pesto, 55
Picatta, Chicken, 130
Pork
  Asian Style, 120
  Bronk Style, 120
  Cajun Style, 119
  Cooking, 120
  Ground - Meatballs, 36
  Maple Ham Glaze, 127
  New Orleans, 119
  Tourtiere, 122
Prosciutto, 12
Puff Pastry, 15
Red Onion Confit, 163
Red Onion Marmalade, 163
Rice Vinegar, 59
Salad
  Curried Corn, 69
  Roast Beef Salad, 25
  Spinach with Raspberry Dressing, 63
  Spinach with Warm Bacon Dressing, 62

White Mountain Salad with Creole Dressing, 66
**Salmon**
Smoked Salmon Mousse, 34
with Tarragon Sauce, 101
Sauce
Basic Tomato Sauce, 146
BBQ, 121
Curry, 87
Puttanesca, 155
Puttanesca, 154, 155
Red Wine and Mushroom, 118
Thai Dipping, 105
Sausage
Italian, 55
Seafood
Calamari Cacciatore, 107
Calamari dipping sauce, 105
Lobster Bisque, 103
Lobster, boiled in Wine, 102
Shrimp Scampi Quesadillas, 19
Shrimp, 19
Garlic, 96
Notes on Shrimp, 93
Shrimp Scampi Quesadillas, 19
Soup
Avocado Gazpacho, 80
Carrot Top Soup, 84
Kale, 82
Lentil with Ham and Potatoes Soup, 80
Roast Squash and Sweet Potato Soup, 76
Roast Squash and Parsnip Soup, 77
Roast Squash and Yellow Tomato Soup, 78
Roasted Beet Soup, 82
Roasted Sweet Potato and Cabbage Soup, 74
Smoked Turkey and Bean Soup, 73
Spinach
Dip with Feta, Lemon and Oregano, 31
Stew
Beef, 72
Tahini, 27
Tapenade, 13
Toasted Sesame Oil, 27
Turkey
Smoked in Bean Soup, 73
Veal
Osso Bucco Ragu, 125
Scaloppini Involtini, 124
Shanks, 126
Vegetables
Beet Greens with Onions and Garlic, 160
Corn and Fennel, 159
Eggplant Stew, 161
Fried Fennel and Onions, 162

Fried Onions & Fennel, 101
Grilled, 55
Grilled, 21
Grilled, 158
Parsnip & Sweet Potato Hash, 157
Parsnips in place of Carrots, 73
Peppers with Anchovies Andalusian style, 99
Potatoes Catalan, 164
Red Onion Confit, 163
Red Onion Marmalade, 163
Red Pepper, Roasting, 132
Sauteed Kale, 160
Spinach with Onions and Garlic, 160
Sweet Potato & Parsnip Hash, 157
Sweet Potato Bread, 50
Waffles, 46
Walnuts, 18
Walnuts, candied, 65
White Mountains Seafood Chowder Fish, 88
Wine
  Barolo, 37, 126, 154, 168
  Cabernet Sauvignon, 14, 25, 73, 112, 113, 114, 116, 117, 118, 119, 136, 167
  Cava, 97
  Chardonnay, 16, 17, 19, 34, 65, 67, 76, 84, 89, 90, 97, 98, 101, 102, 103, 104, 129, 130, 132, 133, 141, 142, 144, 150, 159, 166
  Chianti Classico, 25, 37, 55, 126, 154, 161
  Dry Manzanilla, 97
  Gewurztraminer, 18, 166
  Malbec, 26
  Merlot, 15, 21, 40, 81, 112, 113, 114, 116, 119, 122, 124, 126, 135, 161, 167
  Montecillo, 97
  Pinot Grigio, 12, 32, 62, 64, 79, 100, 166
  Pinot Noir, 15, 19, 38, 87, 138, 168
  Red Wine and Mushroom Sauce, 118
  Rioja, 11, 21, 97
  Sauvignon Blanc, 12, 62, 64, 105, 166
  Sherry, 141
  Shiraz, 26, 168
  Vouvray, 17, 18, 33, 77, 90, 91, 98, 129, 132, 144, 157, 158, 159, 166
  Zinfandel, 10, 14, 26, 40, 55, 72, 73, 112, 113, 114, 116, 117, 119, 124, 135

Made in the USA
Charleston, SC
11 August 2011